Letter to the Student

IT HAS BEEN BUT A CENTURY AND A SCORE — A MERE EYEBLINK OF TIME TO ANY

historian or philosopher—since psychological science began on a December, 1879 day in Wilhelm Wundt's lab. Since that day, we have learned that our neural fabric is composed of separate cells that "talk" to one another through chemical messengers; that our brain's two hemispheres serve differing functions; and that we assemble a simple visual perception by an amazingly intricate process that is rather like taking a house apart, splinter by splinter, and reassembling it elsewhere. We have also learned much about the heritability of various traits, about the roots of misery and happiness, and about the remarkable abilities of newborns. We have learned how abilities vary and how they change with age, how we construct memories, how emotions influence health, how we view and affect one another, and how culture and other environmental factors influence us.

Despite this exhilarating progress, our knowledge may, another century and a score from now, seem to our descendants like relative ignorance. Questions remain unanswered, issues unresolved. What will molecular genetics contribute to our understanding of schizophrenia? What are the relative effects of genetic heritage, home environment, and peers on the personalities and values of developing children? To what extent are our judgments and behaviors the product of thinking that is self-controlled and conscious versus automatic and unconscious? What is the function of dreams? How does the material brain give rise to consciousness?

Psychology is less a set of findings than a way of asking and answering such questions. Over the years, this process of asking and answering questions about behavior and the mind has nowhere been better displayed than in the pages of SCIENTIFIC AMERICAN and its newer sister magazine, SCIENTIFIC AMERICAN: MIND. In this collection from their recent issues, leading scientists—"Magellans of the mind"—show us how they explore and map the mind. They ask, how, from ancient history to the present, have humans understood the brain? How does the brain change with age? How does it enable our perceptions of music, our memories, our language, our intelligence, our disorders? How are we influenced by television, by persuasion, and by our abundance of choices?

In each case, we find a detective story, marked by the testing of competing ideas. "Truth is arrived at by the painstaking process of eliminating the untrue," said master detective Sherlock Holmes. What remains—the apparent truth—is sometimes surprising. "Life is infinitely stranger than anything which the mind of man could invent," Sherlock also declared. So read on, looking not only for the answers, but also for the sleuthing. Therein lies the heart of psychology.

David G. Myers
Hope College
davidmyers.org

Contents

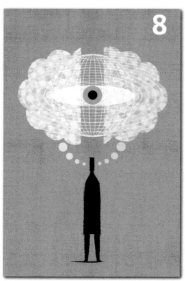
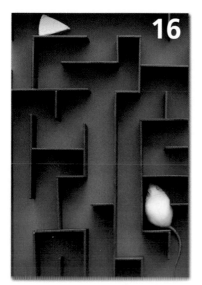

Contents

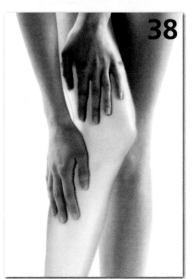

Contents

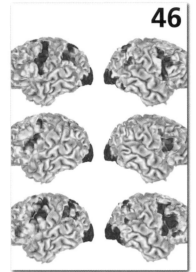

Contents

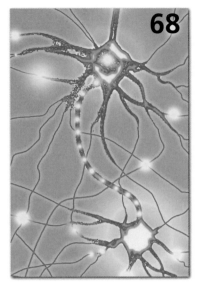

Contents

Contents

Drawing from both his research and his infiltration of sales and fundraising organizations, Robert Cialdini identifies six "weapons of influence." By harnessing some combination of these persuasion principles, people often persuade others to buy, deal, vote, or give. And by making us aware of these tactics, Cialdini aims to make us more mindful and self-directed when someone employs them on us.

DISCUSSION QUESTIONS:

1) From your own observation and experience, what are some examples of these persuasion principles?

2) How might you employ these principles for positive purposes? When are they ethical and appropriate, and when unethical and inappropriate?

Inside the Mind of a Savant

Kim Peek—the inspiration for *Rain Man*—possesses one of the most extraordinary memories ever recorded. Until we can explain his abilities, we cannot pretend to understand human cognition

By Darold A. Treffert and Daniel D. Christensen

When J. Langdon Down first described savant syndrome in 1887, coining its name and noting its association with astounding powers of memory, he cited a patient who could recite Edward Gibbon's *The Decline and Fall of the Roman Empire* verbatim. Since then, in almost all cases, savant memory has been linked to a specific domain, such as music, art or mathematics. But phenomenal memory is itself the skill in a 54-year-old man named Kim Peek. His friends call him "Kim-puter."

He can, indeed, pull a fact from his mental library as fast as a search engine can mine the Internet. Peek began memorizing books at the age of 18 months, as they were read to him. He has learned 9,000 books by heart so far. He reads a page in eight to 10 seconds and places the memorized book upside down on the shelf to signify that it is now on his mental "hard drive."

Peek's memory extends to at least 15 interests—among them, world and American history, sports, movies, geography, space programs, actors and actresses, the Bible, church history, literature, Shakespeare and classical music. He knows all the area codes and zip codes in the U.S., together with the television stations serving those locales. He learns the maps in the front of phone books and can provide MapQuest-like travel directions within any major U.S. city or between any pair of them. He can identify hundreds of classical compositions, tell when and where each was composed and first performed, give the name of the composer and many biographical details, and even discuss the formal and tonal components of the music. Most intriguing of all, he appears to be developing a new skill in middle life. Whereas before he could merely talk about music, for the past two years he has been learning to play it.

It is an amazing feat in light of his severe developmental problems—characteristics shared, in varying extents, by all savants. He walks with a sidelong gait, cannot button his

Kim Peek stands in front
of an image of his brain.

clothes, cannot manage the chores of daily life and has great difficulties with abstraction. Against these disabilities, his talents—which would be extraordinary in any person—shine all the brighter. An explanation of how Peek does what he does would provide better insight into why certain skills, including the ordinarily obscure skill of calendar calculating (always associated with massive memory), occur with such regularity among savants. Recently, when an interviewer offered that he had been born on March 31, 1956, Peek noted, in less than a second, that it was a Saturday on Easter weekend.

Imaging studies of Peek's brain thus far show considerable structural abnormality [*see box on page 6*]. These findings cannot yet be linked directly to any of his skills; that quest is just beginning. Newer imaging techniques that plot the brain's functions—rather than just its structure—should provide more insight, though. In the meantime, we believe it is worthwhile to document the remarkable things that Peek can do. People like him are not easily found, and savantism offers a unique window into the mind. If we cannot explain it, we cannot claim full understanding of how the brain functions.

An Unusual Brain

Peek was born on November 11, 1951. He had an enlarged head, on the back of which was an encephalocele, or baseball-size "blister," which spontaneously resolved. But there were also other brain abnormalities, including a malformed cerebellum. One of us (Christensen) did the initial MRI brain scans on Peek in 1988 and has followed his progress ever since.

The cerebellar findings may account for Peek's problems with coordination and mobility. But more striking still is the absence of a corpus callosum, the sizable stalk of nerve tissue that normally connects the left and right halves of the brain. We do not know what to make of this defect, because, although it is rare, it is not always accompanied by functional disorders. Some people lack the structure without suffering from any detectable problems at all. Yet in people whose corpus callosum has been severed in adulthood, generally in an effort to prevent epileptic seizures from spreading from one hemisphere to the other, a characteristic "split-brain" syndrome arises in which the estranged hemispheres begin to work almost independently of each other.

It would seem that those born without a corpus callosum somehow develop back channels of communication between the hemispheres. Perhaps the resulting structures allow the two hemispheres to function, in certain respects, as one giant hemisphere, putting normally separate functions under the same roof, as it were. If so, then Peek may owe some of his talents to this particular abnormality. In any case, the fact that some people lacking a corpus callosum suffer no disabilities, whereas others have savant abilities, makes its purpose less clear than formerly thought. Neurologists joke that its only two certain functions are to propagate seizures and hold the brain together.

Theory guides us in one respect. Peek's brain shows abnormalities in the left hemisphere, a pattern found in many savants. What is more, left hemisphere damage has been invoked as an explanation of why males are much more likely than females to display not only savantism but also dyslexia, stuttering, delayed speech, and autism. Also supporting the role of left hemisphere damage are the many reported cases of "acquired savant syndrome," in which older children and adults suddenly develop savant skills after damage to the left hemisphere.

What does all this evidence imply? One possibility is that when the left hemisphere cannot

FAST FACTS
Peek's Peaks

1 ›› Savants possess great skills. Kim Peek cannot button his shirt but knows all U.S. zip codes and can recite music he heard only once 40 years ago.

2 ›› Peek's brain is missing a corpus callosum, which connects the hemispheres. This abnormality and others evoke a key question: In development, does the brain compensate for damage or does damage simply allow latent abilities to emerge?

3 ›› Rote learning eventually developed into associative thinking for Peek, with creativity that has helped him engage the wider world. A savant's skills should never be dismissed but should be cultivated for the person's intellectual and social advancement.

ETHAN HILL (*preceding pages*)

function properly, the right hemisphere compensates by developing new skills, perhaps by recruiting brain tissue normally earmarked for other purposes. Another possibility is that injury to the left hemisphere merely unveils skills that had been latent in the right hemisphere all along, a phenomenon some have called a release from the "tyranny" of the dominant left hemisphere.

Peek underwent psychological testing in 1988. His overall IQ score was 87, but the verbal and performance subtests varied greatly, with some scores falling in the superior range of intelligence and others in the mentally retarded range. The psychological report concluded, therefore, that "Kim's IQ classification is not a valid description of his intellectual ability." The "general intelligence" versus "multiple intelligences" debate rages on in psychology. We believe that Peek's case argues for the latter point of view.

Peek's overall diagnosis was "developmental disorder not otherwise specified," with no diagnosis of autistic disorder. Indeed, although autism is more commonly linked with savantism than is any other single disorder, only about half of all savants are autistic. In contrast with autistic people, Peek is outgoing and quite personable. One thing that does seem necessary for the full development of savant skills is a strong interest in the subject matter in question.

Memory and Music

In Peek's case, all the interests began in rote memorization but later progressed to something more. Although Peek generally has a limited capacity for abstract or conceptual thinking—he cannot, for example, explain many commonplace proverbs—he does comprehend much of the material he has committed to memory. This degree of comprehension is unusual among savants. Down himself coined the interesting phrase "verbal adhesion" to describe the savant's ability to remember huge quantities of words without comprehension. Sarah Parker, a graduate student in psychology at the University of Pennsylvania, in a description of a savant named Gordon stated it more colorfully when she noted that "owning a kiln of bricks does not make one a mason." Peek not only owns a large kiln of bricks, he has also become a strikingly creative and versatile word mason within his chosen areas of expertise.

Sometimes his answers are quite concrete and literal. Once when asked by his father in a restaurant to "lower his voice," Peek merely slid lower into his chair, thus lowering his voice box. In other cases, his answers can seem quite ingenious. In

one of his talks he answered a question about Abraham Lincoln's Gettysburg Address by responding, "Will's house, 227 North West Front Street. But he stayed there only one night—he gave the speech the next day." Peek intended no joke, but when his questioner laughed, he saw the point; since then, he has purposely recycled the story with humorous intent and effect.

Peek does have the power to make clever connections. He once attended a Shakespeare festival sponsored by a philanthropist known by the initials O.C., whose laryngitis threatened to keep him from acknowledging a testimonial. Peek—a fan of Shakespeare, and like him, an incorrigible punster—quipped, "O.C., can you say?"

Such creative use of material that had originally been memorized by rote can be seen as the verbal equivalent of a musician's improvisation. Like the musician, Peek thinks quickly, so quickly that it can be difficult to keep up with his intri-

Peek reads a page in eight to 10 seconds, learning it by heart as he goes. His mental library of 9,000 books includes encyclopedic coverage of everything from Shakespeare to musical composers to the maps of all major U.S. cities.

(The Authors)

DAROLD A. TREFFERT and DANIEL D. CHRISTENSEN have long been fascinated by savantism. Treffert, a psychiatrist in Wisconsin, has done research on autism and savant syndrome since 1962, the year he first met a savant. He was consultant to the movie *Rain Man* and is author of *Extraordinary People: Understanding Savant Syndrome*. Christensen is clinical professor of psychiatry, clinical professor of neurology and adjunct professor of pharmacology at the University of Utah Medical School.

ETHAN HILL

cate associations. Often he seems two or three steps ahead of his audiences in his responses.

A rather startling new dimension to Peek's savant skills has recently surfaced. In 2002 he met April Greenan, professor of music at the University of Utah. With her help, he soon began to play the piano and to enhance his discussion of compositions by playing passages from them, demonstrating on the keyboard many of the pieces he recalled from his massive mental library. Peek also has remarkable long-term memory of pitch, remembering the original pitch level of each composition.

He readily identifies the timbre of any instrumental passage. For example, he presented the opening of Bedrich Smetana's orchestral tone poem *The Moldau* by reducing the flute and clarinet parts to an arpeggiated figure in his left hand on the piano. And he explained that the oboes and bassoons enter with the primary theme, which he then reduced to pitches played singly and then in thirds by his right hand (the left-hand figure continuing as it does in the score). His comprehension of musical styles is demonstrated in his ability to identify composers of pieces he had not previously heard by assessing the piece's musical style and deducing who that composer might be.

Though Peek is still physically awkward, his manual dexterity is increasing. When seated at the piano, he may play the piece he wishes to dis-

A Missing Connection?

Kim Peek's brain (*bottom right*) differs from typical brains (*diagram* and *top right*) in several ways. Peek's brain and head are very large, each in the 99th percentile. Most striking is the complete absence of the corpus callosum, which normally connects the left and right hemispheres. Missing, too, are the anterior and posterior commissures, which also link the hemispheres. The cerebellum, responsible for certain motor functions, is smaller than usual and malformed, with fluid occupying much of the surrounding space; this may explain some of Peek's difficulties with coordination. What role these abnormalities play in his mental abilities is being investigated.

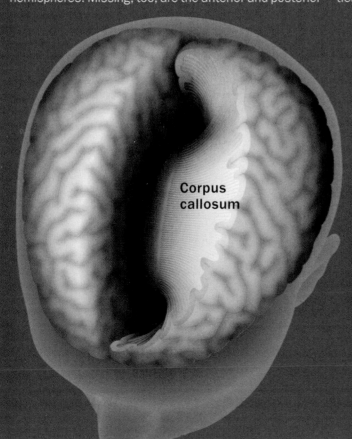

Corpus callosum

Normal brain

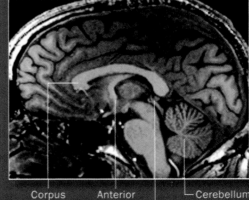

Corpus callosum   Anterior commissure   Cerebellum

Posterior commissure

Kim Peek's brain

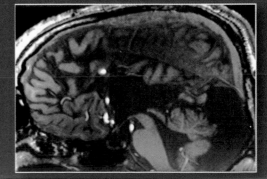

SARA CHEN (*Illustration*); PRATIK MUKHERJEE AND DONNA R. ROBERTS *University of California, San Francisco* (*MRI scans*)

cuss, sing the passage of interest or describe the music verbally, shifting seamlessly from one mode to another. Peek pays attention to rhythm as well, lightly tapping the beat on his chest with his right hand or, when playing, tapping his right foot.

Greenan, a Mozart scholar, makes these observations: "Kim's ability to recall every detail of a composition he has heard—in many cases only once and more than 40 years ago—is astonishing. The connections he draws between and weaves through compositions, composer's lives, historical events, movie soundtracks and thousands of facts stored in his database reveal enormous intellectual capacity." She even compares him to Mozart, who also had an enlarged head, a fascination with numbers and uneven social skills. She wonders whether Peek might even learn to compose.

Life after *Rain Man*

It is not surprising that Peek's prodigious memory caught the attention of writer Barry Morrow at a chance meeting in 1984 and inspired him to write the screenplay for *Rain Man*, whose main character, Raymond Babbitt, is a savant played by Dustin Hoffman. The movie is purely fictional and does not tell Peek's life story, even in outline. But in one remarkably prescient scene, Raymond instantly computes square roots in his head, and his brother, Charlie, remarks, "He ought to work for NASA or something." For Peek, such a collaboration might well happen.

NASA has proposed to make a high-resolution 3-D anatomical model of Peek's brain architecture. Richard Boyle, director of the NASA BioVIS Technology Center, describes the project as part of a larger effort to fuse image data from as wide a range of brains as possible. The data, both static and functional, should enable investigators to identify changes in the brain that accompany thought and behavior. NASA hopes that this detailed model will enable physicians to improve their ability to interpret output from far less capable ultrasound imaging systems, which are the only kind that can now be carried into space to monitor astronauts.

The filming of *Rain Man* and the movie's subsequent success was a turning point in Peek's life. Before then, he had been reclusive, retreating to his room when company came; afterward, the confidence he gained from his contacts with the filmmakers, together with the celebrity provided by the movie's success, inspired him and his father, Fran Peek, to share Kim's talents with many audiences. They became enthusiastic emissaries for people with disabilities, and they have shared their story with more than 2.6 million people.

We believe that Peek's transformation has general applicability. Much of what scientists know about health comes from the study of pathologies, and certainly much of what will be learned about normal memory will come from studying unusual memory. In the meantime, we draw some practical conclusions for the care of persons with special needs who have some savant skill. We recommend that family and other caregivers "train the talent," rather than dismissing such skills as frivolous, as a means for the savant to connect with other people and mitigate the effects of the disability. It is not an easy path, because disability and limitations still require a great deal of dedication, patience and hard work—as Peek's father, by his example, so convincingly demonstrates.

Further exploration of savant syndrome will provide both scientific insights and stories of immense human interest. Kim Peek provides ample evidence of both. **M**

Piano playing is Peek's most recently acquired skill, one at which he is becoming increasingly adept despite having poor coordination. Music professor April Greenan (*seated*) and Peek's father, Fran, have encouraged his efforts.

(**Further Reading**)
◆ **The Real Rain Man.** Fran Peek. Harkness Publishing Consultants, 1996.
◆ **Extraordinary People: Understanding Savant Syndrome.** Updated edition. Darold A. Treffert. iUniverse, Inc., 2006.
◆ **www.savantsyndrome.com**, a Web site maintained by the Wisconsin Medical Society.

ETHAN HILL

Spheres of INFLUENCE

SPLIT-BRAIN PATIENTS—WHOSE TWO HEMISPHERES ARE SEPARATED SURGICALLY—PROVIDE FASCINATING CLUES TO HOW A UNITARY SENSE OF CONSCIOUSNESS EMERGES FROM THE FURIOUS ACTIVITY OF BILLIONS OF BRAIN CELLS BY MICHAEL S. GAZZANIGA

The human brain has approximately 100 billion neurons, and each, on average, connects to about 1,000 other neurons. A quick multiplication reveals that there are 100 trillion synaptical connections. So how is all this input getting spliced and integrated into a coherent package? How do we get order out of this chaos of connections? Even though it may not always seem so, our consciousness is rather kicked back and relaxed when you think about all the input with which the brain is being bombarded and all the processing that is going on. In fact, it is as if our consciousness is out on the golf course like the CEO of a big company while all the underlings are working. It occasionally listens to some chatter, makes a decision and then is out sunning itself.

We have gotten some clues about how consciousness emerges from studying "split brain" patients. The surgical procedure to cut the corpus callosum is a last ditch treatment effort for patients with severe intractable epilepsy for whom no other treatments have worked. Very few patients have had this surgery, and it is done even more rarely now because of improved medications and other modes of treatment. In fact, there have only been 10 split-brain patients who have been well tested. William Van Wagenen, a Rochester, N.Y., neurosurgeon, performed the procedure for the first time in 1940, following the ob- servation that one of his patients with severe seizures got relief after developing a tumor in his corpus callosum. Epileptic seizures are caused by abnormal electrical discharges that in some people spread from one hemisphere to the other. It was thought that if the connection between the two sides of the brain were cut, then the electrical impulses causing the seizures would not spread from one side of the brain to the other. The great

fear was what the side effects of the surgery might be. Would it create a split personality with two brains in one head?

In fact, the treatment was a great success. Most patients' seizure activity decreased 60 to 70 percent, and they felt just fine: no split personality, no split consciousness. Most seemed completely unaware of any changes in their mental processes. This was great, but puzzling nonetheless. Why don't split-brain patients have dual consciousness? Why aren't the two halves of the brain conflicting over which half is in charge? Is one half in charge? Are consciousness and the sense of self actually located in one half of the brain?

Split-brain patients will do subtle things to compensate for their loss of brain connectivity. They may move their heads to feed visual infor-

mation to both hemispheres, or talk out loud for the same purpose, or make symbolic hand movements. Only under experimental conditions, when we eliminate cross cueing, does the disconnection between the two hemispheres become apparent. We are then able to demonstrate the different abilities of the two hemispheres.

Before we see what is separated after this surgery, we need to understand what continues to be shared. There are subcortical pathways that remain intact. Both hemispheres of the split-brain patient are still connected to a common brain stem, so both sides receive much of the same sensory and proprioceptive information automatically coding the body's position in space. Both hemispheres can initiate eye movements, and the brain stem supports similar arousal levels, so both sides sleep and wake up at the same time.

There also appears to be only one integrated spatial-attention system, which continues to be unifocal after the brain has been split. Attention cannot be distributed to two spatially disparate locations. The left brain is not attentive to the blackboard while the right brain is checking out the hot dude in the next row. Emotional stimuli presented to one hemisphere will still affect the judgment of the other hemisphere.

You may have been taught in anatomy lectures that the right hemisphere of the brain controls the left half of the body and that the left hemisphere controls the right half of the body. Of spheres interact quite differently in their control of reflexive and voluntary attention processes. There is a limited amount of overall available attention. The evidence suggests that reflexive (bottom-up) attention-orienting happens independently in the two hemispheres, whereas voluntary attention-orienting involves hemispheric competition with control preferentially lateralized to the left hemisphere. The right hemisphere, however, attends to the entire visual field, whereas the left hemisphere attends only to the right field. When the right inferior parietal lobe is damaged, the left parietal lobe remains intact.

WHY DON'T SPLIT-BRAIN PATIENTS HAVE DUAL CONSCIOUSNESS? WHY AREN'T THE TWO HALVES OF THE BRAIN CONFLICTING OVER WHICH HALF IS IN CHARGE? IS ONE HALF IN CHARGE?

course, things are not quite that simple. For instance, both hemispheres can guide the facial and proximal muscles, such as those in the upper arms and legs, but the separate hemispheres have control over the distal muscles (those farthest from the center of the body), so that the left hemisphere controls the right hand. Although both hemispheres can generate spontaneous facial expressions, only the dominant left hemisphere can do so voluntarily. Because half the optic nerve crosses from one side of the brain to the other at the optic chiasm, the information from the parts of both eyes that attend to the right visual field is processed in the left hemisphere, and vice versa. This information does not cross over from one disconnected hemisphere to the other. If the left visual field sees something in isolation from the right, only the right side of the brain has access to that visual information.

It has also been known since the first studies by French neuroanatomist Paul Broca that our language areas are usually located in the left hemisphere (with exceptions in a few left-handed people). A split-brain patient's left hemisphere and language center have no access to the information that is being fed to the right brain. Bearing these things in mind, we have designed ways of testing split-brain patients to better understand what is going on in the separate hemispheres and have verified and learned that the left hemisphere is specialized for language, speech and intelligent behavior, whereas the right is specialized for such tasks as recognizing upright faces, focusing attention and making perceptual distinctions.

Where attention is concerned, the hemi-

Yet the left parietal lobe directs its visual attention only to the right side of the body. There is no brain area paying attention to what is going on in the left visual field. The question that is left is, Why doesn't this bother the patient? I'm getting there....

Left Hemisphere and Intelligence

After the human cerebral hemispheres have been disconnected, the verbal IQ of a patient remains intact, and so does his problem-solving capacity. There may be some deficits in free-recall capacity and in other performance measures, but isolating essentially half of the cortex from the dominant left hemisphere causes no major change in cognitive functions. The left hemisphere remains unchanged from its preoperative capacity, yet the largely disconnected, same-size right

FAST FACTS
Lessons from Split Brains

1 >> A singular feeling of consciousness emerges from the chaos of 100 trillion neural connections. How?

2 >> "Split brain" patients—whose two hemispheres have been surgically sundered—have given scientists some ideas about how these semi-independent processing modules normally work together to create a unified experience.

3 >> The two hemispheres approach problem-solving situations in complementary ways, with the right able to maintain an accurate record of events and the left focusing on interpretation of those events.

hemisphere is seriously impoverished in cognitive tasks. Although the right hemisphere remains superior to the isolated left hemisphere for some perceptual and attentional skills, and perhaps also emotions, it is poor at problem solving and many other mental activities.

The difference between the two hemispheres in problem solving is captured in a probability-guessing experiment. We have subjects try to guess which of two events will happen next: Will it be a red light or a green light? Each event has a

findings. They have shown the right hemisphere does frequency-match when presented with stimuli for which it is specialized, such as in facial recognition, and the left hemisphere, which is not a specialist in this task, responds randomly. This division of labor suggests that one hemisphere cedes control of a task to the other hemisphere, if the other hemisphere specializes in that task. The left hemisphere, on the other hand, engages in the human tendency to find order in chaos and persists in forming hypotheses about the sequence of

THE LEFT BRAIN, OBSERVING THE LEFT HAND'S RESPONSE WITHOUT THE KNOWLEDGE OF WHY IT HAS PICKED THAT ITEM, HAS TO EXPLAIN IT. IT WILL NOT SAY, "I DON'T KNOW."

different probability of occurrence (for example, a red light appears 75 percent of the time, and a green 25 percent of the time), but the order of occurrence of the events is entirely random.

There are two possible strategies one can use: frequency matching or maximizing. Frequency matching would involve guessing red 75 percent of the time and guessing green 25 percent of the time. The problem with that strategy is that because the order of occurrence is entirely random it can result in a great deal of error—being correct only 50 percent of the time—although it could result in being correct 100 percent of the time as well. The second strategy, maximizing, involves simply guessing red every time. That ensures an accuracy rate of 75 percent because red appears 75 percent of the time. Animals such as rats and goldfish maximize. The "house" in Las Vegas maximizes. Humans, on the other hand, match. The result is that nonhuman animals perform better than humans in this task.

Use of this suboptimal strategy by people has been attributed to a propensity to try to find patterns in sequences of events even when they are told that the sequences are random. At Dartmouth College, psychologists George Wolford, Michael Miller and I tested the two hemispheres of split-brain patients to see if the different sides used the same or different strategies. We found that the left hemisphere used the frequency-matching strategy, whereas the right hemisphere maximized! Our interpretation was that the right hemisphere's accuracy was higher than the left's because the right hemisphere approaches the task in the simplest possible manner with no attempt to form complicated hypotheses about the task.

More recent tests have even more interesting

events even in the face of evidence that no pattern exists: slot machines, for instance. Why does the left hemisphere do this even when it can be non-adaptive?

Know-It-All Left Hemisphere

Several years ago we observed something about the left hemisphere that was very interesting: we had elicited from the disconnected right hemisphere how it deals with behaviors about which it had no information. We showed a split-brain patient two pictures: a chicken claw was shown to his right visual field, so only the left hemisphere saw that, and a snow scene was shown to the left visual field, so the only right hemisphere saw that. He was then asked to choose from an array of pictures placed in full view in front of him. Of the pictures placed in front of the subject, the shovel was chosen with the left hand and the chicken with the right. When asked why he chose these items, his left hemisphere speech center replied, "Oh, that's simple. The chicken claw goes with the chicken, and you need a shovel to clean out the chicken shed." Here the left brain, observing the left hand's response without the knowledge of why it has picked that item, has to explain it. It will not say, "I don't know." Instead it interprets that response in a context consistent with what it knows, and all it knows is "chicken claw." It knows nothing about the snow scene, but it has got to explain that shovel in the left hand. It has to create order out of its behavior. We called this left-hemisphere process "the interpreter."

We also tried the same type of test with mood shifts. We showed a command to the right hemisphere to laugh. The patient began to laugh. Then we asked the patient why she was laughing. The

speech center in the left hemisphere had no knowledge of why its person was laughing, but out would come an answer anyway: "You guys are so funny!" When we triggered a negative mood in the right hemisphere by a visual stimulus, the patient denied seeing anything but suddenly said that she was upset and that it was the experimenter who was upsetting her. She *felt* the emotional response to the stimulus—all the autonomic results—but had no idea what caused it. Ah, lack of knowledge is of no importance, the left brain will find a solution. Order must be made. The first plausible explanation will do: the experimenter did it! The left-brain interpreter makes sense out of all the other processes. It takes all the input that is coming in and puts it together in a makes-sense story, even though it may be completely wrong.

The Interpreter and Consciousness

So here we are, back to the leading question of the article. Why do we feel unified when we are made up of a gazillion modules? Decades of split-brain research have revealed the specialized functions of the two hemispheres and have provided insights into specialization within each hemisphere. The answer may lie in the left-hemisphere interpreter and its drive to seek explanations for why events occur.

In 1962 Stanley Schachter of Columbia Uni-

(The Author)

MICHAEL S. GAZZANIGA is director of the SAGE Center for the Study of the Mind at the University of California, Santa Barbara, and the Summer Institute in Cognitive Neuroscience at Dartmouth College. He serves on the President's Council on Bioethics.

versity and Jerome E. Singer of Pennsylvania State University injected epinephrine into subjects participating in a research experiment. Epinephrine activates the sympathetic nervous system, and the result is an increased heart rate, hand tremors and facial flushing. The subjects were then put into contact with a confederate who behaved in either a euphoric or an angry manner. The subjects who were informed about the effects of the epinephrine attributed symptoms such as a racing heart to the drug. The subjects who were not informed, however, attributed their autonomic arousal to the environment. Those who were paired with the euphoric confederate reported being elated and those with the angry confederate reported being angry. This finding illustrates the human tendency to generate explanations for events. When aroused, we are driven to explain why. If there is an obvious explanation, we accept it, as did the group in-

formed about the effects of epinephrine. When there is not an obvious explanation, the left brain generates one. This is a powerful mechanism; once seen, it makes one wonder how often we are victims of spurious emotional-cognitive correlations. ("I am feeling good! I must really like this guy!" As he is thinking: "Ah, the chocolate is working!")

Although the left hemisphere seems driven to interpret events, the right hemisphere shows no such tendency. A reconsideration of hemispheric-memory differences suggests why this dichotomy might be adaptive. When a person is asked to decide whether a series of items appeared in a study set or not, his or her right hemisphere is able to identify correctly items that have been seen previously and to reject new items. "Yes, there was the plastic fork, the pencil, the can opener and the orange." The left hemisphere, however, tends to falsely recognize new items when they are similar to previously presented items, presumably because they fit into the schema it has constructed. "Yes, the fork (but it is a silver one and not plastic), the pencil (although this one is mechanical, and the other was not), the can opener and the orange." This finding is consistent with the hypothesis that the left-hemisphere interpreter constructs theories to assimilate perceived information into a comprehensible whole.

By going beyond simply observing events to asking why they happened, a brain can cope with such events more effectively should they happen again. In doing so, however, the process of elaborating (story-making) has a deleterious effect on the accuracy of perceptual recognition, as it does with verbal and visual material. Accuracy remains high in the right hemisphere, however, because it

sometimes there really is a conspiracy. In an intact brain, both these cognitive styles are available and can be implemented depending on the situation.

The difference in the way the two hemispheres approach the world might also provide some clues about the nature of human consciousness. In the media, split-brain patients have been described as having two brains. The patients themselves, however, claim that they do not feel any different after the surgery than they did before. They do not have any sense of the dual consciousness implied by the notion of having two brains. How is it that two isolated hemispheres give rise to a single consciousness? The left-hemisphere interpreter may be the answer. The interpreter is driven to generate explanations and hy-

THE DIFFERENCE IN THE WAY THE TWO HEMISPHERES APPROACH THE WORLD MIGHT ALSO PROVIDE SOME CLUES ABOUT THE NATURE OF HUMAN CONSCIOUSNESS.

does not engage in these interpretive processes. The advantage of having such a dual system is obvious. The right hemisphere maintains an accurate record of events, leaving the left hemisphere free to elaborate and make inferences about the material presented. In an intact brain, the two systems complement each other, allowing elaborative processing without sacrificing veracity.

The probability-guessing paradigm also demonstrates why an interpreter in one hemisphere and not the other would be adaptive. The two hemispheres approach problem-solving situations in two different ways. The right hemisphere bases its judgments on simple frequency information, whereas the left relies on the formation of elaborate hypotheses. Sometimes it is just a random coincidence. In the case of random events, the right hemisphere's strategy is clearly advantageous, and the left hemisphere's tendency to create nonsensical theories about random sequences is detrimental to performance. This is what happens when you build a theory on a single anecdotal situation: "I vomited all night. It must have been the food was bad at that new restaurant where I ate dinner." This hypothesis would be good if everyone who ate what you ate became ill, but not if it happened to just one person. It may have been the flu or your lunch. In many situations, however, there is an underlying pattern, and in these situations the left hemisphere's drive to create order from apparent chaos would be the best strategy. Coincidences do happen, but

potheses regardless of circumstances. The left hemisphere of split-brain patients does not hesitate to offer explanations for behaviors that are generated by the right hemisphere. In neurologically intact individuals, the interpreter does not hesitate to generate spurious explanations for sympathetic nervous system arousal. In these ways, the left-hemisphere interpreter may generate a feeling in all of us that we are integrated and unified.

A split-brain patient, a human who has had the two halves of his or her brain disconnected from each other, does not find one side of the brain missing the other. The left brain has lost all consciousness about the mental processes managed by the right brain, and vice versa. We don't miss what we no longer have access to. The emergent conscious state arises out of each side's capacity and probably through neural circuits local to the capacity in question. If they are disconnected or damaged, there is no underlying circuitry from which the emergent property arises.

Each of the thousands if not millions of conscious moments that we have reflects one of our networks being "up for duty." These networks are all over the place, not in one specific location. When one finishes, the next one pops up, and the pipe organ–like device plays its tune all day long. What makes emergent human consciousness so vibrant is that our pipe organ has lots of tunes to play, whereas the rat's (for instance) has few. And the more we know, the richer the concert. **M**

Quiet! Sleeping Brain at Work

During slumber, our brain engages in data analysis, from strengthening memories to solving problems

By Robert Stickgold and Jeffrey M. Ellenbogen

I n 1865 Friedrich August Kekulé woke up from a strange dream: he imagined a snake forming a circle and biting its own tail. Like many organic chemists of the time, Kekulé had been working feverishly to describe the true chemical structure of benzene, a problem that continually eluded understanding. But Kekulé's dream of a snake swallowing its tail, so the story goes, helped him to accurately realize that benzene's structure formed a ring. This insight paved the way for a new understanding of organic chemistry and earned Kekulé a title of nobility in Germany.

Although most of us have not been ennobled, there is something undeniably familiar about Kekulé's problem-solving method. Whether deciding to go to a particular college, accept a challenging job offer or propose to a future spouse, "sleeping on it" seems to provide the clarity we need to piece together life's puzzles. But how does slumber present us with answers?

The latest research suggests that while we are peacefully asleep our brain is busily processing the day's information. It combs through recently formed memories, stabilizing, copying and filing them, so that they will be more useful the next day. A night of sleep can make memories resistant to interference from other information and allow us to recall them for use more effectively the next morning. And sleep not only strengthens memories, it also lets the brain sift through newly formed memories, possibly even identifying what is worth keeping and selectively maintaining or enhancing these aspects of a memory. When a picture contains both emotional and unemotional elements, sleep can save the important emotional parts and let the less relevant background drift away. It can analyze collections of memories to discover relations among them or identify the gist of a memory while the unnecessary details fade—perhaps even helping us find the *meaning* in what we have learned.

Not Merely Resting

If you find this news surprising, you are not alone. Until the mid-1950s, scientists generally assumed that the brain was shut down while we snoozed. Although German psychologist Hermann Ebbinghaus had evidence in 1885 that

RICK GAYLE *Corbis* (head and gears); GETTY IMAGES (background)

The mystery of what happens during sleep has provoked many theories over the centuries.

lows a 90-minute cycle, in and out of rapid-eye-movement (REM) sleep. During REM sleep, our brain waves—the oscillating electromagnetic signals that result from large-scale brain activity—look similar to those produced while we are awake [*see illustration on opposite page*]. And in subsequent decades, the late Mircea Steriade of Laval University in Quebec and other neuroscientists discovered that individual collections of neurons were independently firing in between these REM phases, during periods known as slow-wave sleep, when large populations of brain cells fire synchronously in a steady rhythm of one to four beats each second. So it became clear that the sleeping brain was not merely "resting," either in REM sleep or in slow-wave sleep. Sleep was doing something different. Something *active*.

Sleep to Remember

The turning point in our understanding of sleep and memory came in 1994 in a groundbreaking study. Neurobiologists Avi Karni, Dov Sagi and their colleagues at the Weizmann Institute of Science in Israel showed that when volunteers got a night of sleep, they improved at a task that involved rapidly discriminating between objects they saw—but only when they had had normal amounts of REM sleep. When the subjects were deprived of REM sleep, the improvement disappeared. The fact that performance actually rose overnight negated the idea of passive protection. Something had to be happening within the sleeping brain that altered the memories formed the day before. But Karni and Sagi described REM sleep as a permissive state—one that *could* allow changes to happen—rather than a necessary one. They proposed that such unconscious improvements could happen across the day or the night. What was important, they argued, was that improvements could only occur during *part* of the night, during REM.

It was not until one of us (Stickgold) revisited this question in 2000 that it became clear that sleep could, in fact, be necessary for this improvement to occur. Using the same rapid visual discrimination task, we found that only with more than six hours of sleep did people's performance improve over the 24 hours following the learning session. And REM sleep was not the only important component: slow-wave sleep was equally crucial. In other words, sleep—in all its phases—does something to improve memory that being awake does not do.

To understand how that could be so, it helps to review a few memory basics. When we "en-

sleep protects simple memories from decay, for decades researchers attributed the effect to a passive protection against interference. We forget things, they argued, because all the new information coming in pushes out the existing memories. But because there is nothing coming in while we get shut-eye, we simply do not forget as much.

Then, in 1953, the late physiologists Eugene Aserinsky and Nathaniel Kleitman of the University of Chicago discovered the rich variations in brain activity during sleep, and scientists realized they had been missing something important. Aserinsky and Kleitman found that our sleep fol-

FAST FACTS
While We Are Sleeping

1 ›› As we snooze, our brain is busily processing the information we have learned during the day.

2 ›› Sleep makes memories stronger, and it even appears to weed out irrelevant details and background information so that only the important pieces remain.

3 ›› Our brain also works during slumber to find hidden relations among memories and to solve problems we were working on while awake.

THE SLEEP OF REASON PRODUCES MONSTERS, BY FRANCISCO GOYA. © BRITISH MUSEUM/ART RESOURCE, NY

code" information in our brain, the newly minted memory is actually just beginning a long journey during which it will be stabilized, enhanced and qualitatively altered, until it bears only faint resemblance to its original form. Over the first few hours, a memory can become more stable, resistant to interference from competing memories. But over longer periods, the brain seems to decide what is important to remember and what is not—and a detailed memory evolves into something more like a story.

In 2006 we demonstrated the powerful ability of sleep to stabilize memories and provided further evidence against the myth that sleep only passively (and, therefore, transiently) protects memories from interference. We reasoned that if sleep merely provides a transient benefit for memory, then memories after sleep should be, once again, susceptible to interference. We first trained people to memorize pairs of words in an A-B pattern (for example, "blanket-window") and then allowed some of the volunteers to sleep.

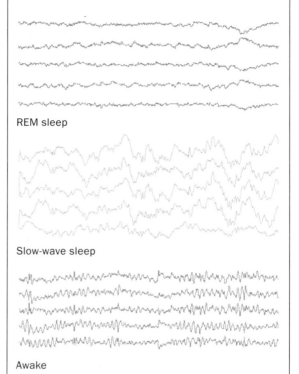

REM sleep

Slow-wave sleep

Awake

The discovery in 1953 of rapid-eye-movement sleep and its characteristic brain activity (*top*), detected with electro-encephalography, dispelled the notion that the brain simply rests during sleep. Soon after, slow-wave sleep patterns (*middle*) were discovered.

(Sleep, it seems, does something to **improve memory** that being awake does not do.)

Later they all learned pairs in an A-C pattern ("blanket-sneaker"), which were meant to interfere with their memories of the A-B pairs. As expected, the people who slept could remember more of the A-B pairs than people who had stayed awake could. And when we introduced interfering A-C pairs, it was even more apparent that those who slept had a stronger, more stable memory for the A-B sets. Sleep changed the memory, making it robust and more resistant to interference in the coming day.

But sleep's effects on memory are not limited to stabilization. Over just the past few years, a number of studies have demonstrated the sophistication of the memory processing that happens during slumber. In fact, it appears that as we sleep, the brain might even be dissecting our memories and retaining only the most salient details. In one study we created a series of pictures that included either unpleasant or neutral objects on a neutral background and then had people view the pictures one after another. Twelve hours later we tested their memories for the objects and the backgrounds. The results were quite surprising. Whether the subjects had stayed awake or slept, the accuracy of their memories

dropped by 10 percent for everything. Everything, that is, except for the memory of the emotionally evocative objects after a night of sleep. Instead of deteriorating, memories for the emotional objects actually seemed to improve by a few percent overnight, showing about a 15 percent improvement relative to the deteriorating backgrounds. After a few more nights, one could imagine that little but the emotional objects would be left. We know this culling happens over time with real-life events, but now it appears that sleep may play a crucial role in this evolution of emotional memories.

Precisely how the brain strengthens and enhances memories remains largely a mystery, although we can make some educated guesses at the basic mechanism. We know that memories are created by altering the strengths of connections among hundreds, thousands or perhaps even millions of neurons, making certain *patterns* of activity more likely to recur. These patterns of activity, when reactivated, lead to the recall of a memory—whether that memory is where we left the car keys or a pair of words such as "blanket-window." These changes in synaptic strength are thought to arise from a molecular process known as long-term potentiation, which strengthens the connections between pairs of neurons that fire at the same time. Thus, cells that fire together wire together, locking the pattern in place for future recall.

During sleep, the brain reactivates patterns of neural activity that it performed during the day, thus strengthening the memories by long-term potentiation. In 1994 neuroscientists Matthew Wilson and Bruce McNaughton, both then at the University of Arizona, showed this effect for the first time using rats fitted with implants that

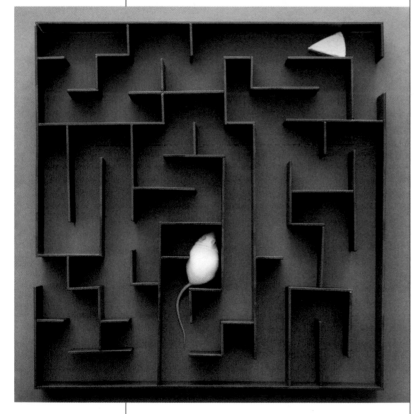

monitored their brain activity. They taught these rats to circle a track to find food, recording neuronal firing patterns from the rodents' brains all the while. Cells in the hippocampus—a brain structure critical for spatial memory—created a map of the track, with different "place cells" firing as the rats traversed each region of the track [see "The Matrix in Your Head," by James J. Knierim; SCIENTIFIC AMERICAN MIND, June/July 2007]. Place cells correspond so closely to exact physical locations that the researchers could monitor the rats' progress around the track

simply by watching which place cells were firing at any given time. And here is where it gets even more interesting: when Wilson and McNaughton continued to record from these place cells as the rats slept, they saw the cells continuing to fire in the same order—as if the rats were "practicing" running around the track in their sleep.

As this unconscious rehearsing strengthens memory, something more complex is happening as well—the brain may be selectively rehearsing the more difficult aspects of a task. For instance, Matthew P. Walker's work at Harvard Medical School in 2005 demonstrated that when subjects learned to type complicated sequences such as 4-1-3-2-4 on a keyboard (much like learning a new piano score), sleeping between practice sessions led to faster and more coordinated finger movements. But on more careful examination, he found that people were not simply getting faster overall on this typing task. Instead each subject was getting faster on those particular keystroke sequences at which he or she was worst.

The brain accomplishes this improvement, at least in part, by moving the memory for these sequences overnight. Using functional magnetic resonance imaging, Walker showed that his subjects used different brain regions to control their typing after they had slept [*see box on opposite page*]. The next day typing elicited more activity in the right primary motor cortex, medial prefrontal lobe, hippocampus and left cerebellum— places that would support faster and more precise key-press movements—and less activity in the parietal cortices, left insula, temporal pole and frontopolar region, areas whose suppression indicates reduced conscious and emotional effort. The entire memory got strengthened, but especially the parts that needed it most, and sleep was doing this work by using different parts of the brain than were used while learning the task.

Solutions in the Dark

These effects of sleep on memory are impressive. Adding to the excitement, recent discoveries show that sleep also facilitates the active analysis of new memories, enabling the brain to solve problems and infer new information. In 2007 one of us (Ellenbogen) showed that the brain learns while we are asleep. The study used a transitive inference task; for example, if Bill is older

When a rat runs a maze, neurons in its brain called place cells are active as it traverses specific regions of the track. Later, as the rat sleeps, the same neurons fire—the rat rehearses its run of the maze while unconscious.

Nocturnal Practice

When pianists learn a new score, they practice difficult runs again and again until the motions become second nature. Part of this internalizing process depends on sleep: a 2005 functional MRI study showed that when people snooze after they learn to type complicated sequences, different brain regions become involved in controlling the keystrokes.

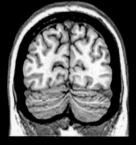 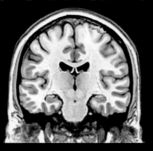 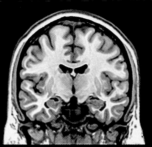 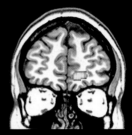

| Left cerebellum | Right primary motor cortex | Right hippocampus | Right medial prefrontal cortex |

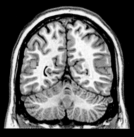 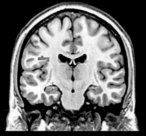 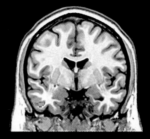 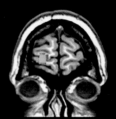

| Parietal lobes | Left insula | Left temporal pole | Left fronto-polar area |

The brain regions indicated in yellow were more active during practice sessions after a night of sleep. These areas support faster typing and more precise keyboard movements—and indeed, subjects who slept improved their speed and accuracy more than did subjects who remained awake between rehearsals. The areas highlighted in blue were less active after sleep, indicating a reduction in conscious and emotional effort during the typing task.

than Carol and Carol is older than Pierre, the laws of transitivity make it clear that Bill is older than Pierre. Making this inference requires stitching those two fragments of information together. People and animals tend to make these transitive inferences without much conscious thought, and the ability to do so serves as an enormously helpful cognitive skill: we discover new information (Bill is older than Pierre) without ever learning it directly.

The inference seems obvious in Bill and Pierre's case, but in the experiment, we used abstract colored shapes that have no intuitive relation to one another [*see top illustration on next page*], making the task more challenging. We taught people so-called premise pairs—they learned to choose, for example, the orange oval over the turquoise one, turquoise over green, green over paisley, and so on. The premise pairs imply a hierarchy—if orange is a better choice than turquoise and turquoise is preferred to green, then orange should win over green. But when we

tested the subjects on these novel pairings 20 minutes after they learned the premise pairs, they had not yet discovered these hidden relations. They chose green just as often as they chose orange, performing no better than chance.

When we tested subjects 12 hours later on the same day, however, they made the correct choice 70 percent of the time. Simply allowing time to pass enabled the brain to calculate and learn these transitive inferences. And people who slept during the 12 hours performed significantly better, linking the most distant pairs (such as orange versus paisley) with 90 percent accuracy. So it seems the brain needs time after we learn information to process it, connecting

(The Authors)

ROBERT STICKGOLD is an associate professor at Harvard Medical School and Beth Israel Deaconess Medical Center in Boston. Also at Harvard, JEFFREY M. ELLENBOGEN is chief of the sleep division at Massachusetts General Hospital. Both study the interactions of sleep and cognition.

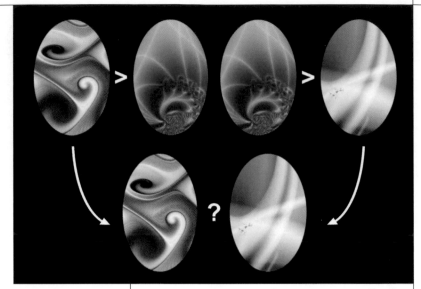

Through trial and error, study volunteers learned that orange is a better choice than turquoise, and turquoise is preferred to green. But only after time did they infer the hidden relation between orange and green, and with harder problems, sleep gave a distinct advantage.

the dots, so to speak—and sleep provides the maximum benefit.

In a 2004 study Ullrich Wagner and others in Jan Born's laboratory at the University of Lübeck in Germany elegantly demonstrated just how powerful sleep's processing of memories can be. They taught subjects how to solve a particular type of mathematical problem by using a long and tedious procedure and had them practice it about 100 times. The subjects were then sent away and told to come back 12 hours later, when they were instructed to try it another 200 times.

What the researchers had not told their subjects was that there is a much simpler way to solve these problems [see box below]. The researchers could tell if and when subjects gained insight into this shortcut, because their speed would suddenly increase. Many of the subjects did, in fact, discover the trick during the second session. But

when they got a night's worth of sleep between the two sessions, they were more than two and a half times more likely to figure it out—59 percent of the subjects who slept found the trick, compared with only 23 percent of those who stayed awake between the sessions. Somehow the sleeping brain was solving this problem, without even knowing that there was a problem to solve.

The Need to Sleep

As exciting findings such as these come in more and more rapidly, we are becoming sure of one thing: while we sleep, our brain is anything but inactive. It is now clear that sleep can consolidate memories by enhancing and stabilizing them and by finding patterns within studied material even when we do not know that patterns might be there. It is also obvious that skimping on sleep stymies these crucial cognitive processes: some aspects of memory consolidation only happen with more than six hours of sleep. Miss a night, and the day's memories might be compromised—an unsettling thought in our fast-paced, sleep-deprived society.

But the question remains: Why did we evolve in such a way that certain cognitive functions happen only while we are asleep? Would it not seem to make more sense to have these operations going on in the daytime? Part of the answer might be that the evolutionary pressures for sleep existed long before higher cognition—functions such as immune system regulation and efficient energy usage (for instance, hunt in the day and rest at night) are only two of the many reasons it makes sense to sleep on a planet that alternates between light and darkness. And because we al-

Sudden Insight

Researchers taught subjects to use two rules to solve a type of problem that consists of a series of ones, fours and nines: Starting from the left, look at the first two numbers. If they are the same, write this number down (*shown here in blue*). If they are different, write down the third possible number (for example, if they are a 1 and a 4, write down 9). Then take this intermediate (*blue*) number and the

next (*black*) number, and do it again. When you enter the final answer (*the red 9 here*), press the "Enter" key to tell the computer you're done.

What the subjects were not told is that the second-to-last unique number in the original series (*the black 9 just before the final 4 in this case*) will always be equivalent to the answer of the problem. After sleeping, most of the volunteers figured out the trick. —*R.S. and J.M.E.*

JEFFREY M. ELLENBOGEN (top)

We may be able to get by on as little as six hours of sleep a night, but closer to eight hours is better— and may optimize learning and memory performance.

ready had evolutionary pressure to sleep, the theory goes, the brain evolved to use that time wisely by processing information from the previous day: acquire by day; process by night.

Or it might have been the other way around. Memory processing seems to be the only function of sleep that actually requires an organism to truly sleep—that is, to become unaware of its surroundings and stop processing incoming sensory signals. This unconscious cognition appears to demand the same brain resources used for processing incoming signals when awake. The brain, therefore, might have to shut off external inputs to get this job done. In contrast, although other functions such as immune system regulation might be more readily performed when an organism is inactive, there does not seem to be any reason why the organism would need to lose awareness. Thus, it may be these other functions that have been added to take advantage of the sleep that had already evolved for memory.

Many other questions remain about our nighttime cognition, however it might have evolved. Exactly how does the brain accomplish this memory processing? What are the chemical or molecular activities that account for these ef-

fects? These questions raise a larger issue about memory in general: What makes the brain remember certain pieces of information and forget others? We think the lesson here is that understanding sleep will ultimately help us to better understand memory.

The task might seem daunting, but these puzzles are the kind on which scientists thrive—and they can be answered. First, we will have to design and carry out more and more experiments, slowly teasing out answers. But equally important, we are going to have to sleep on it. **M**

(Further Reading)

◆ **Visual Discrimination Learning Requires Sleep after Training.** Robert Stickgold, LaTanya James and J. Allan Hobson in *Nature Neuroscience,* Vol. 3, No. 12, pages 1237–1238; December 2000.
◆ **Sleep Inspires Insight.** Ullrich Wagner, Steffen Gais, Hilde Haider, Rolf Verleger and Jan Born in *Nature,* Vol. 427, pages 352–355; January 22, 2004.
◆ **Sleep-Dependent Memory Consolidation.** Robert Stickgold in *Nature,* Vol. 437, pages 1272–1278; October 27, 2005.
◆ **Coordinated Memory Replay in the Visual Cortex and Hippocampus during Sleep.** Daoyun Ji and Matthew Wilson in *Nature Neuroscience,* Vol. 10, No. 1; January 2007.
◆ **Human Relational Memory Requires Time and Sleep.** J. M. Ellenbogen, P. Hu, J. D. Payne, D. Titone and M. P. Walker in *Proceedings of the National Academy of Sciences USA,* Vol. 104, No. 18, pages 7723–7728; May 2007.

JUPITERIMAGES

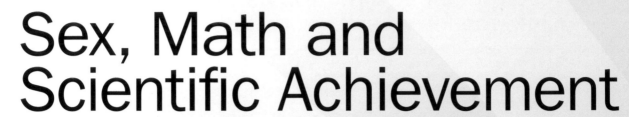

Sex, Math and Scientific Achievement

Why do men dominate the fields of science, engineering and mathematics?

GETTY IMAGES

BY DIANE F. HALPERN, CAMILLA P. BENBOW, DAVID C. GEARY, RUBEN C. GUR, JANET SHIBLEY HYDE AND MORTON ANN GERNSBACHER

For years, blue-ribbon panels of experts have sounded the alarm about a looming shortage of scientists, mathematicians and engineers in the U.S.—making dire predictions of damage to the national economy, threats to security and loss of status in the world. There also seemed to be an attractive solution: coax more women to these traditionally male fields. But there was not much public discussion about the reasons more women are not pursuing careers in these fields until 2005, when then Harvard University president Lawrence Summers offered his personal observations.

He suggested to an audience at a small economics conference near Boston that one of the major reasons women are less likely than men to achieve at the highest levels of scientific work is because fewer females have "innate ability" in these fields. In the wake of reactions to Summers's provocative statement, a national debate erupted over whether

Brains versus brains: Men and women probably have different cognitive strengths as the result of a complex interplay between nature and nurture.

intrinsic differences between the sexes were responsible for the underrepresentation of women in mathematical and scientific disciplines.

As a group of experts with diverse backgrounds in the area of sex differences, we welcome these ongoing discussions because they are drawing the public's attention to this important issue. In this article, we present an analysis of the large body of research literature pertaining to the question of female participation in these fields, information that is central to understanding sex differences and any proposal designed to attract more women to the science and mathematics workforces. Contrary to the implications drawn from Summers's remarks, there is no single or simple answer for why there are substantially fewer women than men in some areas of science and math. Instead a wide variety of factors that influence career choices can be identified, including cognitive sex differences, education, biological influences, stereotyping, discrimination and societal sex roles.

It does not take a Ph.D. to see how making fuller use of female talent would go a long way toward increasing the number of scientific workers. In the U.S., for example, women made up 46 percent of the workforce in 2003 but represented only 27 percent of those employed in science and engineering. One reason Summers's comment upset many people was its implication that any attempt to close this gap was futile. If most women are naturally deficient in scientific ability, then what could be done? But this

FAST FACTS
Closing the Sex Gap

1 >> Women, on average, have stronger verbal skills (especially in writing) and better memory for events, words, objects, faces and activities.

2 >> Men generally are better at mentally manipulating objects and at performing certain quantitative tasks that rely on visual representations.

3 >> Intervention studies are still in their infancy but suggest both sexes can benefit from targeted training to improve their skill set.

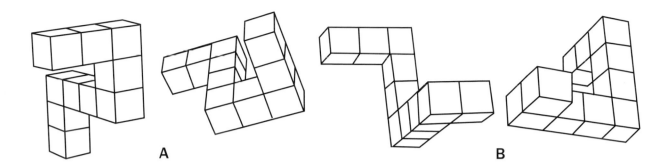

A

B

Defining Sex Differences

seemingly simple interpretation contains two misconceptions.

First, there is no single intellectual capacity that can be called "scientific ability." (For simplicity, we will often use the term "scientific" to refer to skills important to work in the fields of science, technology, engineering and mathematics.) The tools needed for scientific achievement include verbal abilities such as those required to write complex journal articles and communicate well with colleagues; memory skills such as the ability to understand and recall events and complex information; and quantitative abilities in mathematical modeling, statistics, and visualization of objects, data and concepts.

Second, if women and men did demonstrate differences in these talents, this fact would not mean these differences were immutable. Indeed, if training and experience did not make a difference in the development of our academic skills, universities such as Harvard would be accepting tuition from students under false pretenses.

One of the confusing things about the field of sex differences is that you can arrive at very different conclusions depending on how you decide to assess abilities. Women clearly have the right stuff to cut it academically. They have constituted the majority of college enrollments in the U.S. since 1982, with the attendance gap widening every year since then. Similar trends are occurring in many other countries. Furthermore, women receive higher average grades in school in every subject—including mathematics and science.

Despite their success in the classroom, however, women score significantly lower on many standardized tests used for admissions to college and graduate school. The disparity in male-female enrollment in science and related fields grows larger at advanced levels of the education system. For example, in the late 1990s women represented 40 percent of undergraduates in science at the Massachusetts Institute of Technology but only 8 percent of the faculty.

Because grades and overall test scores depend on many factors, psychologists have turned to assessing better-defined cognitive skills to understand these sex differences. Preschool children seem to start out more or less even, because girls and boys, on average, perform equally well in early cognitive skills that relate to quantitative thinking and knowledge of objects in the surrounding environment.

Around the time school begins, however, the sexes start to diverge. By the end of grade school and beyond, females perform better on most assessments of verbal abilities. In a 1995 review of the vast literature on writing skills, University of Chicago researchers Larry Hedges (now at Northwestern University) and Amy Nowell put it this way: "The large sex differences in writing ... are alarming. The data imply that males are, on average, at a rather profound disadvantage in the performance of this basic skill." There is also a female advantage in memory of faces and in episodic memory—memory for events that are personally experienced and are recalled along with information about each event's time and place.

There is another type of ability, however, in which boys have the upper hand, a skill set referred to as visuospatial: an ability to mentally navigate and model movement of objects in three dimensions. Between the ages of four and five, boys are measurably better at solving mazes on standardized tests. Another manifestation of visuospatial skill in which boys excel involves "mental rotation," holding a three-dimensional object in memory while simultaneously transforming it [see illustration above]. As might be expected, these capabilities also give boys an edge in solving math problems that rely on creating a mental image.

Indeed, of all the sex differences in cognitive abilities, variation in quantitative aptitude has received the most media attention. This popular

Men generally perform better at "mental rotation" tasks such as this one. The task is to determine if the two figures labeled A and the two figures labeled B could be made identical by rotating them in space.

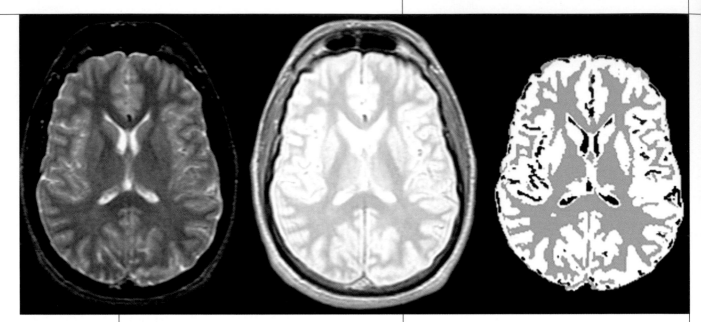

FROM JOURNAL OF NEUROSCIENCE, VOL. 19, NO. 10: MAY 15, 1999; COURTESY OF RUBEN C. GUR

Sexing the brain: A variety of brain-imaging techniques have allowed researchers to find differences in the structure and function of female and male brains.

fascination is, in part, because mastery of these skills is a prerequisite for mathematically intensive disciplines such as physics and engineering. And, as Summers suggested, if women were disadvantaged in these skills, it would go a long way to explaining why women are typically underrepresented in these fields. But the data are much less clear-cut.

As we said before, females get higher grades in math classes at all grade levels and also do slightly better on international assessments in algebra, perhaps because of its languagelike structure. But boys shine on the math part of the Scholastic Aptitude Test (SAT)—resulting in a difference of about 40 points that has been maintained for over 35 years. When all the data on quantitative ability are assessed together, however, the difference in average quantitative ability between girls and boys is actually quite small. What sets boys apart is that many more of them are mathematically gifted.

At first, this statement seems almost paradoxical. If boys and girls are, on average, equally skilled at math, how could there be greater numbers of gifted boys? For reasons that are not yet fully understood, it turns out that males are much more variable in their mathematical ability, meaning that females of any age are more clustered toward the center of the distribution of skills and males are spread out toward the ends. As a result, men outnumber women at the very high—and very low—ends of the distribution. Data from the Study of Mathematically Precocious Youth exemplify this phenomenon. In the 1980s one of us (Benbow), along with the late psychologist Julian C. Stanley, who founded this study at the John Hopkins University Center for

Talented Youth, observed sex differences in mathematical reasoning ability among tens of thousands of intellectually talented 12- to 14-year-olds who had taken the SAT several years before the typical age.

Among this elite group, no significant differences were found on the verbal part of the SAT, but the math part revealed sex differences favoring boys. There were twice as many boys as girls with math scores of 500 or higher (out of a possible score of 800), four times as many boys with scores of at least 600, and 13 times as many boys with scores of at least 700 (putting these test takers in the top 0.01 percent of 12- to 14-year-olds nationwide).

Although it has drawn little media coverage, dramatic changes have been occurring among these junior math wizards: the relative number of girls among them has been soaring. The ratio of boys to girls, first observed at 13 to 1 in the 1980s, has been dropping steadily and is now only about 3 to 1. During the same period the number of women in a few other scientific fields has surged. In the U.S., women now make up half of new medical school graduates and 75 percent of recent veterinary school graduates. We cannot identify any single cause for the increase in the number of women entering these formerly male-dominated fields, because multiple changes have occurred in society over the past several decades.

This period coincides with a trend of special programs and mentoring to encourage girls to take higher-level math and science courses. And direct evidence exists that specifically targeted training could boost female performance even further. A special course created by engineering professor Sheryl A. Sorby and mathematics education specialist Beverly J. Baartmans at Michigan Technological University, for example, targeted improvement in visuospatial skills. All first-year engineering students with low scores on a test of this ability were encouraged to enroll in the course. This enrollment resulted in improved performance in subsequent graphics courses by these students and better retention in engineering programs, which suggests that the effects persisted over time and were of at least some practical significance for both women and men.

tasks such as language processing that call on more symmetric activation of brain hemispheres, whereas males excel in tasks requiring activation of the visual cortex. Even when men and women perform the same task equally well, studies suggest they sometimes use different parts of their brain to accomplish it.

It is important to emphasize, though, that finding sex differences in brain structures and functions does not suggest these are the sole cause of observed cognitive differences between males and females. Because the brain reflects learning and other experiences, it is possible that sex differences in the brain are influenced by the differences in life experiences that are typical for women and men.

> What leads **one little Einstein** to choose electrical engineering and the other law?

The Role of Biology

Decades of data from studies of different animal species show that hormones can play a role in determining the cognitive abilities that males and females develop. For example, during typical prenatal male development, high levels of hormones such as testosterone masculinize the developing brain and result in male-typical behaviors and probably male patterns of cognitive performance.

More recent studies have shown that hormones continue to play a role in cognitive development throughout life. Such changes have been observed in individuals receiving large quantities of male or female hormones in preparation for sex-change surgery. Researchers found, for example, that people undergoing female-to-male hormone treatment show "masculine" changes in their cognitive patterns: improvements in visuospatial processing and decrements in verbal skills.

The human brain is shaped by these hormones, as well as by our genetic inheritance and a lifetime of experiences, so it should not be surprising that numerous differences appear in female and male brains. In general, females have a higher percentage of gray matter brain tissue, areas with closely packed neurons and fast blood flow, whereas males have a higher volume of connecting white matter tissue, nerve fibers that are insulated by a white fatty protein called myelin. Furthermore, men tend to have a higher percentage of gray matter in the left hemisphere, whereas no such asymmetries are significant in females.

Imaging studies assessing brain function support the notion that females perform better on

Ladies' Choice

Of course, even if you're smart, you might not want to be a scientist. Studies of mathematically gifted youth are of special interest to understanding the psychology of career choice because, within this sample, there is little doubt that each boy and girl has the capacity to excel in science. What leads one little Einstein to choose electrical engineering and the other law? A 10-year study of 320 profoundly gifted individuals (top one in 10,000) found that those whose mathematical skills were stronger than their verbal ones (even though they had very high verbal ability) said math and science courses were their favorites and were very likely to pursue degrees in those areas. On the other hand, those kids whose verbal skills were even higher than their math skills said humanities courses were their favorites and most often pursued educational credentials in the humanities and law.

It appears then that highly gifted kids ask themselves, "What am I better at?" rather than

(The Authors)

DIANE F. HALPERN is a psychologist at Claremont McKenna College. CAMILLA P. BENBOW is dean of education and human development at Vanderbilt University. DAVID C. GEARY is a psychologist at the University of Missouri. RUBEN C. GUR is a psychologist at the University of Pennsylvania. JANET SHIBLEY HYDE and MORTON ANN GERNSBACHER are psychologists at the University of Wisconsin–Madison.

Most standardized math tests—such as those of the SAT college admission test—favor male students, even though women receive higher average grades in college math classes.

direction. People's individual expectations for success are shaped by their perception of their own skills. One factor in forming our self-perception is how authority figures such as teachers and parents perceive and respond to us. A 1992 study by psychology professors Lee Jussim of Rutgers University and Jacquelynne Eccles of the University of Michigan at Ann Arbor found that the level at which teachers rated a student's mathematical talent early in the school year predicted later test scores—even when objective measures of ability were at odds with the teacher's perception. This study and others suggest that stereotypes of science as masculine may prejudice educators against girls from the start.

The Enduring Glass Ceiling

Perhaps most troubling is the thought that a skilled, confident scientist could climb to the top and still face discrimination when she gets there. Nevertheless, plenty of research suggests that people's perception of a job as stereotypically masculine or feminine results in a bias in hiring and compensating candidates or employees who are male and female, respectively. Even though social psychologists agree that the overt sexism that existed decades ago in the U.S. and in many other countries is now rare, they say it has been replaced by unconscious sexism in some situations.

The real-world impact of covert biases on female achievement in science is not well studied because of the shroud of secrecy surrounding peer review, the process by which many aspects of a scientist's career—awarding of grants, acceptance of academic papers for publication and decisions about hiring—are judged by a panel of other, often anonymous, scientists.

There has been one thorough study of the real-world peer-review process. Biologists Christine Wenneras and Agnes Wold of Goeteborg University gained access to the Swedish Medical Research Council's data on postdoctoral fellowship awards only after a battle in court. Shortly before the investigators published their study in 1997, the United Nations had named Sweden the leading country in the world with respect to equal opportunities for men and women. Even so, men dominated Swedish science. At the time, women received 44 percent of Swedish biomedical doctoral degrees but held only 25 percent of postdoctoral positions and 7 percent of professional positions.

What Wenneras and Wold discovered was

"Am I smart enough to succeed in a particular career?" This finding provides some insight into sex differences. Among precocious children, boys more frequently exhibit a "tilt" favoring mathematical and related abilities compared with verbal aptitude. Encouraging more balanced gifted students to keep science and technology fields open as options may help top off the pipeline with more high-achieving female and male students.

It is true that multiple psychological and social factors play a part in determining career shocking. Female applicants received lower mean scores in all areas in which they were evaluated: scientific competence, quality of proposed methodology and relevance of the research proposal. It was possible that the women applicants were less qualified. To test this possibility, the investigators computed scientific productivity based on the applicant's total number of publications, number of first-author publications, quality of each publication and number of times other scientific papers cited their work. By these measures, the *most* productive group of female researchers was rated as comparable in ability to the *least* productive male researchers. All other women were rated below all the men. The authors of this study concluded that the peer-review process in what is arguably the most gender-equal nation in the world is rife with sexism. These results provide a strong rationale for making the peer-review process more transparent. Despite these findings, which were published in the top-ranked international scientific journal *Nature,* there has been no progress toward making the peer-review process more open.

Finally, we cannot consider success at work without considering the effort needed for families to function and maintain a home. Even when husbands and wives both work full-time, women continue to assume most of the child care duties and to shoulder most of the responsibility for tending to sick and elderly family members. Women work, on average, fewer hours per week and spend more time on family and household tasks than comparably educated men do. For women, having children is associated with lower income and a reduced probability of attaining tenure. In contrast, men show a slight tendency to benefit professionally when they become fathers. Thus, the different roles women and men play in family care can also explain their differential participation in demanding careers.

Where We Go from Here

If Larry Summers's comments had one appealing feature, it was the benefit of simplicity. If the lack of women in science were a reflection, in part, of lack of ability, then the take-home lesson would seem to be that we can do nothing but accept the natural order of things.

As this article shows, however, the truth is

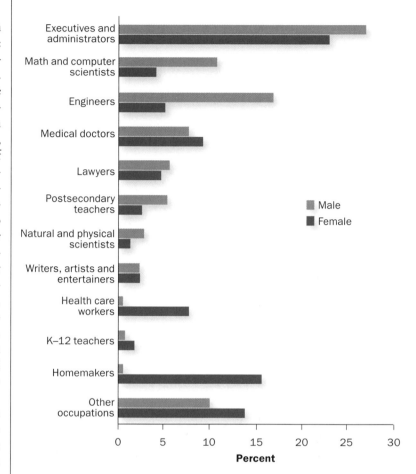

Sex differences in career choice are apparent even among mathematically gifted children. The graph shows a study on the eventual career choice of boys and girls who ranked in the top 1 percent in mathematical ability.

not so simple. Both sexes, on average, have their strengths and weaknesses. Nevertheless, the research argues much could be done to try to help more women—and men for that matter—excel in science and coax them to choose it as a profession. The challenges are many, requiring innovations in education, targeted mentoring and career guidance, and a commitment to uncover and root out bias, discrimination and inequality. In the end, tackling these issues will benefit women, men and science itself. **M**

(Further Reading)

◆ **The Science of Sex Differences in Science and Mathematics.** Diane F. Halpern, Camilla P. Benbow, David C. Geary, Ruben C. Gur, Janet Shibley Hyde and Morton Ann Gernsbacher in *Psychological Science in the Public Interest,* Vol. 8, No. 1, pages 1–51; August 2007.

BY C. P. BENBOW, D. LUBINSKI, D. L. SHEA AND H. EFTEKHARI-SANJANI IN PSYCHOLOGICAL SCIENCE, VOL. 11, NO. 6; 2000

Set *in* Our Ways

Millions of us dream of transforming our lives, but few of us are able to make major changes after our 20s. Here's why

By Nikolas Westerhoff

"The shortest path to oneself leads around the world."

So wrote German philosopher Count Hermann Keyserling, who believed that travel was the best way to discover who you are.

That was how 22-year-old Christopher McCandless was thinking in the summer of 1990, when he decided to leave everything behind—including his family, friends and career plans. He gave his bank balance of $24,000 to the charity Oxfam International and hitchhiked around the country, ending up in Alaska. There he survived for about four months in the wilderness before dying of starvation in August 1992. His life became the subject of writer Jon Krakauer's 1996 book *Into the Wild*, which inspired the 2007 film of the same name.

Not every newly minted college graduate is as impulsive and restless as McCandless was, but studies conducted since the 1970s by personality researchers Paul Costa and Robert R. McCrae of the National Institutes of Health confirm that people tend to be open to new experiences during their teens and early 20s. Young people fantasize about becoming an adventurer like McCandless rather than following in the footsteps of a grandparent who spent decades working for the same company. But after a person's early 20s, the fascination with novelty declines, and resistance to change increases. As Costa and McCrae found, this pattern holds true regardless of cultural background.

Although people typically lose their appetite for novelty as they age, many continue to claim a passion for it. Voters cheer on politicians who pledge change. Dieters flock to nutritional programs advertising a dream figure in only five weeks. Consumers embrace self-help books promising personal transformation. And scientists tell us that novel stimuli are good for our brains, promoting learning and memory [see "Learning by Surprise," on page 35].

Yet even as people older than 30 yearn for what is new, many find themselves unable or unwilling to make fundamental changes in their lives. Researchers say this paradox can be largely explained by the demands of adult responsibilities and that unrealistic expectations may also play a part in thwarting our best intentions. Change is rarely as easy as we think it will be.

The Age of Openness

Psychologists have long identified openness to new experiences as one of the "Big Five" personality traits, which also include extroversion, agreeableness, conscientiousness and neuroticism. Considerable disagreement exists about how much these personality traits change after age 30, but most research suggests that openness declines in adulthood.

THE ROAD NOT TAKEN: For some, the long path to self-discovery begins with expanding one's geographic horizons.

CALL OF THE WILD: To fulfill a dream, 22-year-old Christopher McCandless hitchhiked across the U.S. in the 1990s, making his way to the Alaskan wilderness. His adventurous life was the subject of the film *Into the Wild*, starring Emile Hirsch.

VINCENT BESNAULT Getty Images (*preceding pages*); RIVER ROAD / PARAMOUNT / THE KOBAL COLLECTION (*still from Into the Wild*)

"Clear age trends are observable," says psychologist Peter Borkenau of Martin Luther University Halle-Wittenberg in Germany. "People tend to become more reliable and agreeable with age, but their openness to novelty drops at the same time."

In a comprehensive survey of more than 130,000 participants published in 2003, psychologist Sanjay Srivastava, now at the University of Oregon, and his colleagues assessed the Big Five traits in 21- to 60-year-olds using standard psychological tests on the Internet. They found that openness increased modestly up to age 30 and then declined slowly in both men and women. The survey results suggest that men begin adulthood slightly more open to new experiences than women but decline in openness during their 30s at a faster rate than women.

Age 30 is not a magical turning point, however. Openness declines gradually over many years, often beginning in the 20s. As the years wear on, novelty becomes less and less stimulating, and the world outside someone's own private and professional sanctums becomes increasingly less attractive.

This change happens to almost everyone, regardless of individual personality. That does not mean that everyone reaches the same level of openness in later life, however. Some toddlers love to go back to the same playground day after day, whereas others get bored after a day or two of digging in the same sandbox with the same shovel. Children who are less open to new experiences than their peers are will continue in adulthood to cleave to the conventional more than their more adventurous childhood friends will. As psychologist Richard W. Robins of the University of California, Davis, showed in a longitudinal study, those who begin life with a more open personality remain relatively more open in their later years.

Nature or Nurture?

The fact that an age-dependent pattern of decreasing openness appears around the globe and in all cultures suggests, according to biopsychologists, a genetic basis. But the jury is still out. As psychologist and personality researcher Rainer Riemann of Bielefeld University in Germany points out, it is conceivable that people all over the globe are simply confronted with similar life demands and societal

---

FAST FACTS
Personality through the Years

1 Studies of personality development often focus on traits such as extroversion, conscientiousness, agreeableness, neuroticism and openness to new experiences. In most people, these traits change more during young adulthood than any other period of life, including adolescence. Openness typically increases during a person's 20s and goes into a gradual decline after that.

2 This pattern of personality development seems to hold true across cultures. Although some see that as evidence that genes determine our personality, many researchers theorize that personality traits change during young adulthood because this is a time of life when people assume new roles: finding a partner, starting a family and beginning a career.

3 Personality can continue to change somewhat in middle and old age, but openness to new experiences tends to decline gradually until about age 60. After that, some people become more open again, perhaps because their responsibilities for raising a family and earning a living have been lifted.

Learning by Surprise

Novelty enhances memory. That fact has practical implications for educators

By Daniela Fenker and Hartmut Schütze

You take the same route to work every day, driving the same car, crossing the same intersection with the same median strip. Same old, same old. But this morning something new catches your eye: a cow grazing in the median. It takes a couple of honks to remind you that the light has turned green.

If you are like most people, you will remember this moment in your morning commute for a long time—the sun was shining, daffodils had just pushed up in the median, and "We Are the Champions" was playing on the radio. Yet all the other countless times you have driven through this intersection are long forgotten.

Psychologists have known for some time that if we experience a novel situation within a familiar context, we will more easily store this event in memory. But only recently have studies of the brain begun to explain how this process happens and to suggest new ways of teaching that could improve learning and memory.

Novelty Detector

One of the most important brain regions involved in discovering, processing and storing new sensory impressions is the hippocampus, located in the temporal lobe of the cerebral cortex. Novel stimuli tend to activate the hippocampus more than familiar stimuli do, which is why the hippocampus serves as the brain's "novelty detector."

The hippocampus compares incoming sensory information with stored knowledge. If these differ, the hippocampus sends a pulse of the messenger substance dopamine to the substantia nigra (SN) and ventral tegmental area (VTA) in the midbrain. From there nerve fibers extend back to the hippocampus and trigger the release of more dopamine. Researchers, including John Lisman of Brandeis University and Anthony Grace of the University of Pittsburgh, call this feedback mechanism the hippocampal-SN/VTA loop (*above right*).

This feedback loop is why we remember things better in the context of novelty. As Shaomin Li and his colleagues at Trinity College Dublin discovered in 2003, the release of dopamine in the hippocampus of rats activates the synapses among nerve cells, creating stronger connections that lead to long-term memory storage. We wondered whether this same neuronal loop facilitates the retention of other information that is perceived along with novel stimuli.

At the University of Magdeburg's Institute for Cognitive Neurology, in collaboration with Emrah Düzel and Nico Bunzeck of University College London, we used functional magnetic resonance imaging to measure the activity of various brain regions based on blood flow. We presented one group of test subjects with a set of already known images and a second group with a

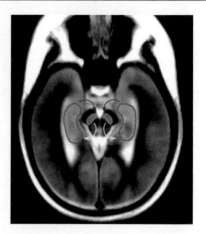

FEEDBACK LOOP: The hippocampus (*circled in blue in brain cross section*) responds to novel stimuli by sending a burst of the messenger substance dopamine (*red*) to the substantia nigra and the ventral tegmental area (SN/VTA; *circled in green*), according to the hippocampal-SN/VTA loop model. From the SN/VTA, nerve fibers run back to the hippocampus (*yellow*), triggering the release of additional dopamine in response to novelty. These brain structures deteriorate with age, which may help account for why seniors sometimes have trouble remembering new information.

combination of known and new images. Subjects in the second group were better at remembering the images than subjects in the first group were, and the fMRI data showed greater activity in the SN and VTA areas of the brain when the subjects were viewing unfamiliar images. This correlation may help explain how novelty improves memory.

Increased Retention

Are the effects of novelty on memory merely temporary? To answer this question, we showed test subjects a variety of photographs and measured their brain activity using fMRI. We also gave the participants a series of words to sort according to their meaning.

The experiment continued the next day when we showed some of the test subjects new images while others viewed familiar ones. Then we asked all the subjects to recall as many words from the previous day's exercise as they could. Recall was significantly better in the group that had just viewed new images.

In other words, novelty seems to promote memory. This finding gives teachers a potential tool for structuring their lessons more effectively. Although most teachers start a lesson by going over material from the previous class before moving on to new subject matter, they should probably do just the opposite: start with surprising new information and then review the older material.

Daniela Fenker and Hartmut Schütze are researchers at the University of Magdeburg's Neurology Clinic II in Germany.

The "Big Five" Personality Traits

In the 1970s two research teams led by Paul Costa and Robert R. McCrae of the National Institutes of Health and Warren Norman and Lewis Goldberg of the University of Michigan at Ann Arbor and the University of Oregon, respectively, discovered that most human character traits can be described using five dimensions. Surveys of thousands of people yielded these largely independent traits:

>> Extroversion The most broadly defined of the Big Five factors measures cheerfulness, initiative and communicativeness. Those who score high for extroversion are companionable, sociable and able to accomplish what they set out to do. Those with low scores tend to be introverted, reserved and more submissive to authority.

>> Openness People with high scores here love novelty and are generally creative. At the other end of the scale are those who are more conventional in their thinking, prefer routines, and have a pronounced sense of right and wrong.

>> Agreeableness This trait describes how we deal with others. High values show that someone is friendly, empathetic and warm. Shy, suspicious and egocentric individuals score low on the spectrum.

>> Conscientiousness This dimension measures a person's degree of organization. Those with high scores are motivated, disciplined and trustworthy. Irresponsible and easily distracted people are found at the low end of the scale.

>> Neuroticism This scale measures emotional stability. People with high scores are anxious, inhibited, moody and less self-assured. Those at the lower end are calm, confident and contented.

Where are you on the Big Five scale? You can find out by taking a free personality test at **www.outofservice.com/bigfive**

—N.W.

expectations. Young men and women everywhere have to go out into the world and find a partner and a livelihood. Later, they have to care for their children and grandchildren. These life tasks require commitment and consistency and may serve as a catalyst for personality change.

Once a family and career are in place, novelty may no longer be as welcome. New experiences may bring innovation and awakening but also chaos and insecurity. And so most people dream of novelty but hold fast to the familiar. Over time we become creatures of habit: enjoying the same dishes when we eat out, vacationing in favorite spots and falling into daily routines [see "Foraging in the Modern World," SCIENTIFIC AMERICAN MIND, Vol. 19, No. 6, 2009].

"The brain is always trying to automate things and to create habits, which it imbues with feelings of pleasure. Holding to the tried and true gives us a feeling of security, safety, and competence while at the same time reducing our fear of the future and of failure," writes brain researcher Gerhard Roth of the University of Bremen in Germany in his 2007 book whose title translates as *Personality, Decision, and Behavior.*

But even negative events may have thoroughly positive results, according to sociologist Deborah Carr of Rutgers University. For example, many widows are able to start life over again and to develop talents they never knew they had. People who have been diagnosed with cancer learn to redefine themselves as a result of the disease—and may even conquer their cancer in the process. Survivors of natural catastrophes often discover new strengths. But we should not draw sweeping conclusions from these examples, says psychologist William R. Miller of the University of New Mexico. Many older people report that they have changed little in spite of major life experiences.

In a recent experiment psychologist Kate C. McLean of the University of Toronto Mississauga asked 134 volunteers of different ages—some older than 65 and others ranging in age from late adolescence through young adulthood—to describe three self-defining memories. She found that both old and young participants reported novel experiences such as the death of a partner, an unexpected career advancement or a cross-country move. The older people ascribed different meanings to these events than the younger people did, however. For younger people, external changes were more likely to lead to internal transformation, but that was not the case for older individuals.

These very different narratives are no coinci-

(The Author)

NIKOLAS WESTERHOFF has a doctorate in psychology and is a science journalist in Berlin.

NICOLAS MONU iStockphoto

dence. Personality traits change more during young adulthood than any other period of life, according to psychologist Brent W. Roberts of the University of Illinois, who together with two colleagues analyzed 92 studies of personality development. They concluded that some personality changes occur well past the age of 30 but that typically these changes are small in magnitude compared with the changes that occur between the ages of 20 and 40.

Even major life events such as a divorce or the death of a loved one, though stressful, are unlikely to result in profound personality changes. The middle years of life are often a time of reflection and reevaluation, but few people experience a genuine "midlife crisis."

The structure of one's personality becomes increasingly stable until about age 60. "That means that a person who is particularly conscientious at the age of 40 will be conscientious at 60 as well," Borkenau says. Stability decreases again, however, after the age of 60. It seems that people are only able to become more open to new experiences once they have fulfilled their life obligations—that is, after they have retired from their careers and their children have flown the nest.

False Hope Springs Eternal

Even after age 60 it is difficult to completely reframe your life. In fact, those who seek to make large changes often end up failing even to make the most minor corrections. The more an individual believes he can set his own rudder as he pleases, the more likely he is to run aground. That's one reason why so many smokers who tell you that they can quit whenever they want are still smoking 20 years later.

In 1999 psychologists Janet Polivy and C. Peter Herman of the University of Toronto Mississauga coined a term for this phenomenon: false hope syndrome. Over and over, they say, people undertake both small and large changes in their lives. Most of these attempts never get anywhere, thanks to overblown expectations [see "Picture Imperfect," by David Dunning, Chip Heath and Jerry M. Suls; SCIENTIFIC AMERICAN MIND, Vol. 16, No. 4, 2005].

Take the woman who believes that if she can lose 20 pounds she will finally meet the man of her dreams and live happily ever after. This fantasy is based on the notion that one positive change—losing weight—automatically brings with it other desired changes. But the reality is that it is difficult to keep weight off over the long term, and finding an ideal life partner is often dependent on luck. Even if dieting proves successful, other goals may remain

HIGH FLIERS: Paragliding, parachuting and bungee jumping are a welcome change from the daily routine for some—for others, a nightmare.

out of reach. But the false hope syndrome seduces people into trying to overhaul their entire lives all at once: the smoker and couch potato is suddenly inspired to become a nonsmoker and marathon runner, but because he attempts too much too fast, he is doomed to fail.

The cure for false hope is to set more reasonable goals and recognize that achieving even modest change will be difficult. And if you are older than 30, remember that your openness to new experiences is slowly declining, so you are better off making a new start today than postponing it until later. Perhaps most important of all, try to appreciate the person that you already are.

As the ancient Greek philosopher Epicurus put it: "Do not spoil what you have by desiring what you have not; but remember that what you now have was once among the things only hoped for." **M**

(Further Reading)

- **Into the Wild.** Jon Krakauer. Villard Books, 1996.
- **Personality at Midlife: Stability, Intrinsic Maturation, and Response to Life Events.** Paul T. Costa, Jr., Jeffrey H. Herbst, Robert R. McCrae and Ilene C. Siegler in *Assessment,* Vol. 7, No. 4, pages 365–378; December 2000.
- **Development of Personality in Early and Middle Adulthood: Set Like Plaster or Persistent Change?** Sanjay Srivastava, Oliver P. John, Samuel D. Gosling and Jeff Potter in *Journal of Personality and Social Psychology,* Vol. 84, No. 5, pages 1041–1053; 2003.
- **Patterns of Mean-Level Change in Personality Traits across the Life Course: A Meta-analysis of Longitudinal Studies.** Brent W. Roberts, Kate E. Walton and Wolfgang Viechtbauer in *Psychological Bulletin,* Vol. 132, No. 1, pages 1–25; January 2006.
- **Stories of the Young and the Old: Personal Continuity and Narrative Identity.** Kate C. McLean in *Developmental Psychology,* Vol. 44, No. 1, pages 254–264; January 2008.

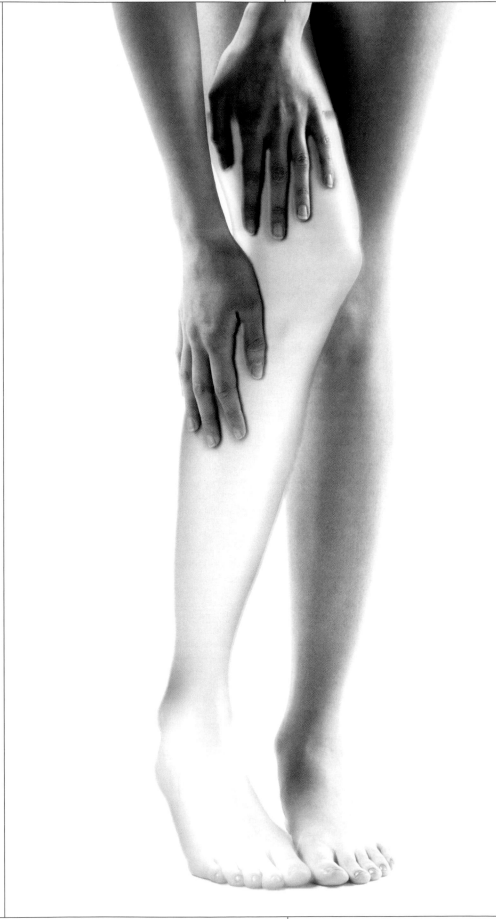

Living with *Ghostly* Limbs

Scientists are pinpointing the neurological roots of the vivid and painful illusion of phantom limbs in amputees—and finding ways to curb it

By Miguel Nicolelis

One morning in my fourth year of medical school, a vascular surgeon at the University Hospital in São Paulo, Brazil, invited me to visit the orthopedics inpatient ward. "Today we will talk to a ghost," the doctor said. "Do not get frightened. Try to stay calm. The patient has not accepted what has happened yet, and he is very shaken."

A boy around 12 years old with hazy blue eyes and blond curly hair sat before me. Drops of sweat soaked his face, contorted in an expression of horror. The child's body, which I now watched closely, writhed from pain of uncertain origin. "It really hurts, doctor; it burns. It seems as if something is crushing my leg," he said. I felt a lump in my throat, slowly strangling me. "Where does it hurt?" I asked. He replied: "In my left foot, my calf, the whole leg, everywhere below my knee!"

As I lifted the sheets that covered the boy, I was stunned to find that his left leg was half-missing; it had been amputated right below the knee after being run over by a car. I suddenly realized that the child's pain came from a part of his body that no longer existed. Outside the ward I heard the surgeon saying, "It was not him speaking; it was his phantom limb."

At that time, I did not know that at least 90 percent of amputees—millions worldwide—have experienced a phantom limb: the strange and errant feeling that a missing body part is still present and attached to their body. In some cases, the part moves; in others, it is locked in place. Such ghostly appendages are often defined by a diffuse tingling sensation that extends throughout the amputated limb

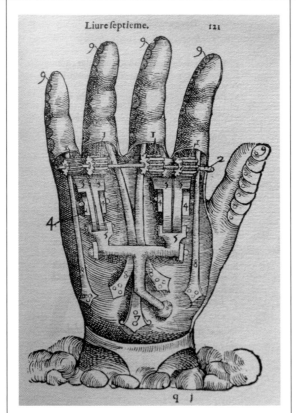

Liure septieme.   121

Artificial articulated hand designed by French military surgeon Ambroise Paré, who described many cases of phantom limbs in soldiers returning from European battlefields in the 1500s. His work was ignored for more than 300 years.

and effectively reconstructs it. These phantoms are often very painful and terrifyingly vivid. In some cases, they endure for years.

Although scientists are still struggling to identify the biological basis for such apparitions, recent research suggests that they are not the product of erroneous neural signals emanating from an amputee's stump. Rather, most neuro-scientists now believe, they arise largely from activity in networks of neurons distributed throughout the brain. These networks enable a person to create an anatomical image of his or her own body and attach sensations to that body image. Studies of such cerebral representations and how they change after amputation have led to new experimental therapies for phantom limb syndrome.

Painful Appendages

Scientists, doctors and laypeople have known about phantom limbs for centuries. During the Middle Ages, for instance, European folklore glorified the miraculous restoration of sensation in amputated limbs in soldiers.

In one account, which dates back to the fourth century, twin boys tried to physically reattach limbs onto patients who had lost an arm or leg. The amputees supposedly developed the feeling of the divine presence in the missing part of their body—presumably the result of a phantom. The boys later became official saints of the Catholic Church; amputees who prayed to their memory felt their limbs coming back. In the 1500s French military surgeon Ambroise Paré, whose improved surgical techniques boosted survival for amputees, described many cases of the phenomenon in soldiers returning from European battlefields.

In 1872 American neurologist Silas Weir Mitchell coined the term "phantom limb" to describe the sensations that mutilated Civil War soldiers felt in their lost limbs. Since then, scientists have written up hundreds of case studies, revealing various manifestations. Interviews with amputees suggest that intense limb pain before amputation, say, from a severe fracture, deep ulcer, burn or gangrene, is a major risk factor for developing phantom pain afterward—as if the pain were etched in memory so that it remains even after its source is gone. More than 70 percent of patients find their phantom limbs painful immediately after surgery; in many cases, the pain persists for years.

Phantom limbs sometimes perform phantom movements. Recent amputees may even wake up screaming that their nonexistent leg is "trying to leave the bed on its own to walk around the room." In one third of afflicted people, however, the absent limb becomes completely paralyzed, often agonizingly so—for instance, embedded in an ice cube, permanently twisted in a spiral or tortuously pinned to the back.

Researchers now know that phantom sensa-

FAST FACTS
Anatomical Apparitions

1 >> At least 90 percent of amputees have had a phantom limb: they perceive that a missing body part is still present and attached to their body. Such phantoms are often very painful and may persist for years.

2 >> Recent studies suggest that phantom limbs are not the product of erroneous neural signals emanating from an amputee's stump. Rather they are now thought to arise largely from activity in neural networks in the brain that build a mental image of the body.

3 >> Researchers are trying to treat phantom limb syndrome using mirrors and virtual reality, both of which create illusions that can help patients gain better control over their ghostly appendages and may help decrease phantom pain.

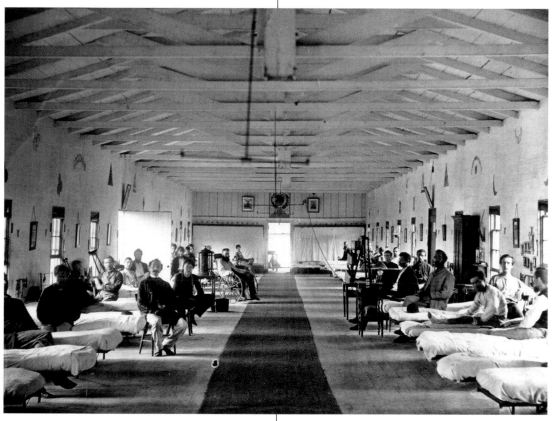

Armory Square Hospital, Washington, D.C., 1865. American neurologist Silas Weir Mitchell coined the term "phantom limb" to describe the sensations that Civil War soldiers felt in their lost limbs.

tions can occur in any excised body part, not just the arms and legs; people who have lost their breasts, teeth, genitals and even internal organs have had them. Women with hysterectomies, for example, have felt illusory menstrual pain and laborlike uterine contractions.

Pain from phantom limbs can also be very debilitating. Amputees with such pain are much less likely to use a prosthetic limb, studies have shown, restricting their ability to care for themselves, visit friends and engage in other activities. And unfortunately, only a tiny fraction of such patients find relief from the dozens of available pain therapies.

Blaming the Brain

Despite decades of investigation, scientists have not pinned down the biological origins of this disturbing illusion. An early notion, put forth during the second half of the 20th century, came from the late neuroscientist Patrick Wall, then at University College London. Wall placed blame for the phantom limb phenomenon on the severed nerve fibers in the scarred region of the amputee's stump. These fibers form nodules, or neuromas, which were thought to send erroneous signals through the spinal cord to the brain that might be misinterpreted as tingling or pain in the absent limb.

When doctors attempted to treat phantom limb sensations by cutting the sensory nerves leading to the spinal cord, severing nerves in the cord, or even removing parts of the brain that receive the sensory neuronal tracts, the phantoms nonetheless persisted. Sometimes the patients' pain temporarily vanished but then returned. Thus, many researchers rejected the idea that problems with the peripheral nerves could fully account for the syndrome.

In the late 1980s psychologist Ronald Melzack of McGill University and his colleagues put forth the alternative notion that illusory body parts arise at least in part from neural activity within the brain. Such a view echoed earlier writings from naturalist Erasmus Darwin, an 18th-century British intellectual and grandfather to Charles Darwin, who once penned: "Does it not seem clear that such a [phantom]

The Body in the Brain

The brain not only receives sensory signals from various parts of the body, but it is thought to generate its own pattern of neural activity that represents the body in its intact state. The brain's somatosensory cortex contains a map of various body regions; it receives tactile information from the body via a sensory pathway that traverses the thalamus. Another neural conduit transmits information from the body to the limbic system, which governs emotions such as those associated with phantom limbs. After the loss of a body part, activity in this neural system may result in the perception of a phantom limb.

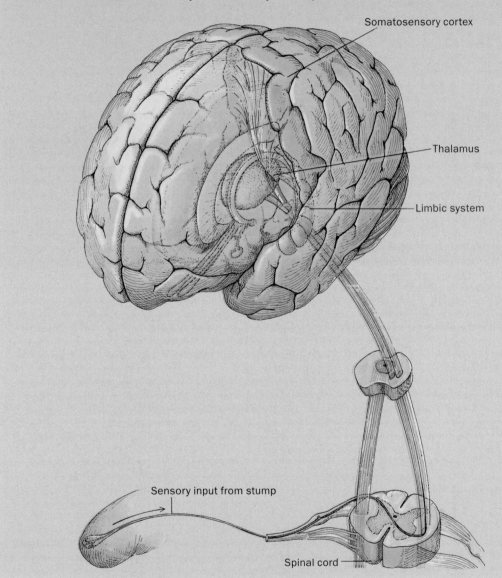

Somatosensory cortex

Thalamus

Limbic system

Sensory input from stump

Spinal cord

phenomenon indicates that our ideas and sensations emerge from our brains, and not from our tactile organs?"

In Melzack's view, the brain not only detects sensory signals from the body but also generates its own neural pattern, or neural signature, that represents the body in its intact state. This signature inscribes the psyche with a sense of the body's configuration and borders—and of the body belonging to an individual. It persists even after the removal of a body part, creating the mistaken perception that the part is still present and attached to the body.

Orchestrating such a neural signature, the theory goes, falls to a large network of neurons that Melzack termed the "neuromatrix." The neuromatrix includes the somatosensory cortex at the brain's surface on the top of the head and other regions of the parietal lobe (a quadrant of the brain beneath the top and back of the head) that construct a person's body image and his or her sense of self. In addition, it consists of two neural pathways: the sensory pathway that conveys tactile information through the thalamus— a sensory relay station deep in the brain—to the somatosensory cortex and another that traverses the brain's limbic system, a group of buried brain structures that govern emotions such as those associated with phantom limbs [*see box on opposite page*].

Consistent with such a theory, damage to part of this neuromatrix can result in the loss of ownership of part or all of one's body. (It might also result in body integrity identity disorder [see "Amputee Envy," by Sabine Mueller, Scientific American Mind, Dec 2007/Jan 2008].) Injuries to the right parietal lobe caused by brain trauma or stroke can lead to left hemibody neglect syndrome, in which patients become indifferent to the entire left side of their body. Such patients may, for example, fail to put on the left sleeve of a shirt or a left shoe. When asked about such behavior, these individuals typically deny that the left arm or leg is theirs; the counterpart to the right side of their body, they assert, belongs to someone else.

The effect can be transient in some cases— and very strange. In one instance described to me, a NASA astronaut piloting his first space mission told his colleagues during the initial orbit to "stop poking their hands in his left control panel." His crew informed him that the hand in question was his own, but the pilot denied it, declaring that "the hand in the left panel is certainly not mine." A few hours later, to the relief of the crew (and Houston), the pilot suddenly said, "Just relax, guys. I have found my missing left hand on the control panel!" Presumably, the spacecraft's acceleration during liftoff or the lack of gravity temporarily deprived the pilot's right parietal lobe of blood, producing a fleeting form of left hemibody neglect syndrome.

Modifying the Matrix

The basic structure of our neuromatrix may be present at birth, its blueprint likely inscribed in our genes, Melzack proposes. Such a congeni-

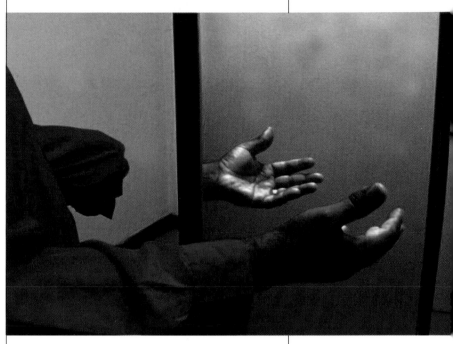

tal network would explain why, as Melzack and his colleagues reported in 1997, phantom arms or legs often appear in children born without these body parts. Melzack's team found phantoms in 41 of 125 people who were either born without a limb or had one amputated before age six, indicating that such anatomical ghosts occur in about a fifth of people missing a limb at birth and more than half of amputees who are young children. Thus, the human brain seems able to generate a neural picture of the complete human physique even in the absence of sensory signals from the body.

Nevertheless, gross changes in body structure after birth—and, consequently, neural input to the neuromatrix—can provoke changes in this brain network, some of which may buttress the brain's role in creating phantom limbs. The somatosensory cortex in the parietal lobe contains neurons that receive input from, and so are thought to produce a conscious sense of, the various body parts.

A vertical mirror reflecting the image of an intact limb can create the illusion that a phantom limb has been resurrected and can be controlled. Exercises using such a mirror have relieved phantom limb spasms and pain in a small number of amputees.

(The Author)

MIGUEL NICOLELIS is a professor of neurobiology and biomedical engineering at Duke University and coordinator of the Edmond and Lily Safra International Institute of Neurosciences of Natal in Brazil. He also lectures at the Swiss Federal Institute of Technology in Lausanne, Switzerland. He holds an M.D. and a Ph.D. from the University of São Paulo.

COURTESY OF VILAYANUR S. RAMACHANDRAN

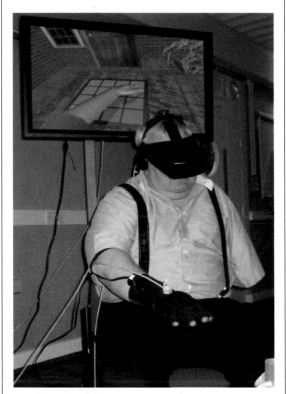

An amputee immerses himself in a three-dimensional virtual reality in which his real limb movements are transposed onto a virtual limb that serves as a stand-in for his phantom limb. In this world, users transfer feelings from their real limb to the muscles and joints of the phantom. A preliminary study suggests that the illusion can result in partial relief of phantom pain.

These neurons are arranged in a topographical map. Experiments conducted in the 1980s by neuroscientists Jon Kaas of Vanderbilt University and Michael Merzenich of the University of California, San Francisco, and their colleagues, among others, have shown that amputation causes a restructuring of this body map such that the cerebral neurons that represented the excised part switch their allegiance to adjacent body regions. Merzenich's team, for example, found that amputation of a monkey's middle finger caused the brain cells that previously responded only to stimulation of that finger to respond instead to stimulation of the index and ring fingers within a matter of months.

In 1993 John Chapin and I showed that this reorganization process started immediately after blocking impulses from sensory nerves in the whiskers of rats and that it occurred in the thalamus, among other deeper brain structures, as well as the somatosensory cortex. The late neuroscientist Tim Pons, then at the National Institute of Mental Health, and his co-workers extended this idea. Cutting off sensory input from a monkey's entire arm, they found, prompted a more widespread reorganization in which the neurons once assigned to the hand switched to react to signals from the face, which is represented next to the arm in the brain's map. In 1998 they reported a similar reorganization in the thalamus and brain stem relays of the somatosensory system.

Such revamping also occurs in the human cerebral cortex after an arm amputation, according to work by neuroscientist Vilayanur S. Ramachandran of the University of California, San Diego, and his colleagues. Using an imaging technique called magnetoencephalography, which measures the magnetic fields produced by electrical activity in the brain, the researchers showed in the early 1990s that sensory input from the face activated the hand area in the brain's cerebral body map.

When Ramachandran's team touched the faces of amputees in particular locations, the researchers found that the sensory nerve signals, now traveling to the hand area of the somatosensory cortex, evoked feelings in their phantom hand. Moreover, the researchers found that the lower face region contains an organized map of the hand such that tactile stimulation of specific points on the face elicits sensations from specific points on the phantom hand. The type of sensation—whether hot, cold, rubbing or massage—is the same in both locations.

Other efforts have since linked such brain reorganization to phantom limb pain. In a 1995 study neuroscientist Herta Flor of the University of Heidelberg in Germany and her colleagues used noninvasive neuromagnetic techniques to detect the degree of cortical reorganization in 20 amputees. They found a strong relation between the amount of neural restructuring and the magnitude of phantom arm pain, suggesting that the pain may result from such changes in the somatosensory cortex.

A follow-up 2001 study led by psychologist Niels Birbaumer of the University of Tuebingen in Germany lends further support to this idea. The scientists, who included Flor, used a brain-imaging technique called functional magnetic resonance imaging to show that imagined movement of the phantom hand activated the face area of the somatosensory cortex in patients with phantom limb pain, but not in pain-free amputees. The researchers hypothesize that phantom limb pain results from the simultaneous activation of the hand and mouth regions of the brain's body map.

Ghost Busters

Ramachandran and his wife, neuroscientist Diane Rogers-Ramachandran, have since developed a possible treatment for phantom limb syndrome based on the malleability of the brain's body maps. The researchers removed the top of a cardboard box and inserted a vertical mirror. Ten arm amputees inserted their intact arm in the front of the box so that the arm's reflection in the mirror overlay the perceived location of the phantom limb. This created a visual illusion that the phantom arm had been resurrected. When each patient moved his real arm, he could see that his "phantom" arm was obeying his motor commands [see "It's All Done with Mirrors," by Vilayanur S. Ramachandran and Diane Rogers-Ramachandran; SCIENTIFIC AMERICAN MIND, August/September 2007].

Six of the patients who used the mirror box said they could feel as well as see their phantom moving, generating the impression that both arms could now be moved. Four of the patients used this newfound ability to relax and open a clenched phantom hand, which provided relief from painful spasms. Three weeks of daily practice with the mirror caused one patient's phantom arm to largely disappear. And when most of the limb vanished, so did the pain from the phantom elbow. The visual illusion apparently corrected the tactile one, suggesting that the activity of central visual circuits can modify the activity of the proposed neuromatrix, the researchers reported in 1996.

A decade later psychologist Eric Brodie of Glasgow Caledonian University in Scotland and his colleagues reported hints of success in a test of a mirror box modified for a leg. Forty-one lower-limb amputees watched a reflection of their intact leg in the mirror as they moved this leg and tried to move their phantom leg. Another 39 amputees tried to move both their phantom and real legs without the mirror. Both efforts, which involved 10 different movements each repeated 10 times, diminished phantom limb sensations, including pain. Although the mirror did not enhance this effect, it did produce significantly more phantom limb movements and more vivid awareness of the phantom leg than did the exercise without the mirror. Prolonged mirror treatment might be more effective in fighting phantom pain, the researchers propose, perhaps by reversing the ongoing reorganization of the brain thought to be responsible for phantom limb pain.

Researchers are now trying to ameliorate phantom limb pain with immersive three-dimensional computer simulations—so-called virtual reality (VR)—that can produce illusions similar to those created by the mirror. The technology can display a patient's entire body, including his or her phantom limb, and enable the patient to perform complex movements of the fingers, toes, hands, feet, arms and legs that are not possible with mirror therapy. In a preliminary 2007 study psychologist Craig Murray and his colleagues at the University of Manchester in England exposed two upper-limb amputees and one lower-limb amputee to a simulation that transported a user's limb movements to those of a virtual limb, which overlay their phantom limb in the virtual environment. All three amputees, who participated in two to five VR sessions, reported that sensations from their real limb were transferred to the muscles and joints of their phantom limb. In each case, phantom pain decreased during at least one of the sessions, suggesting that such therapy might offer pain relief for these types of patients.

The possibility of such a treatment seemed remote that afternoon in São Paulo, some 25 years ago, when I saw the boy shrieking in pain from a leg he no longer had. If I had known then what I know now, I would have been able to reassure the boy that what he was feeling, however excruciating and strange, was merely a phantasmagoric tactile memory of the past, created in every exquisite and cruel detail by a normally functioning brain—and not by a terrible curse. Perhaps by knowing that, my first patient would have found more bearable such a frightening and undesirable life companion. **M**

(Further Reading)

◆ **The Perception of Phantom Limbs: The D. O. Hebb Lecture.** V. S. Ramachandran and William Hirstein in *Brain*, Vol. 121, Part 9, pages 1603–1630; 1998.

◆ **Analgesia through the Looking Glass? A Randomized Controlled Trial Investigating the Effect of Viewing a "Virtual" Limb upon Phantom Limb Pain, Sensation and Movement.** Eric E. Brodie, Anne Whyte and Catherine A. Niven in *European Journal of Pain*, Vol. 11, No. 4, pages 428–436; published online July 20, 2006.

◆ **Phantom Limbs.** Ronald Melzack in *Scientific American Reports*, Vol. 16, No. 3, pages 53–59; September 2006.

◆ For information about amputation, see www.answers.com/topic/amputation-3?cat=health

MIRRORS IN THE MIND

A special class of brain cells reflects the outside world, revealing a new avenue for human understanding, connecting and learning

By Giacomo Rizzolatti, Leonardo Fogassi and Vittorio Gallese

John watches Mary, who is grasping a flower. John knows what Mary is doing—she is picking up the flower—and he also knows why she is doing it. Mary is smiling at John, and he guesses that she will give him the flower as a present. The simple scene lasts just moments, and John's grasp of what is happening is nearly instantaneous. But how exactly does he understand Mary's action, as well as her intention, so effortlessly?

A decade ago most neuroscientists and psychologists would have attributed an individual's understanding of someone else's actions and, especially, intentions to a rapid reasoning process not unlike that used to solve a logical problem: some sophisticated cognitive apparatus in John's brain elaborated on the information his senses took in and compared it with similar previously stored experiences, allowing John to arrive at a conclusion about what Mary was up to and why.

Although such complex deductive operations probably do occur in some situations, particularly when someone's behavior is difficult to decipher, the ease and speed with which we typically understand simple actions suggest a much more straightforward explanation. In the early 1990s our research group at the University of Parma in Italy, which at the time included Luciano

ACTION PERFORMED by one person can activate motor pathways in another's brain responsible for performing the same action. The second understands viscerally what the first is doing because this mirror mechanism lets her experience it in own her mind.

Fadiga, found that answer somewhat accidentally in a surprising class of neurons in the monkey brain that fire when an individual performs simple goal-directed motor actions, such as grasping a piece of fruit. The surprising part was that these same neurons also fire when the individual sees someone else perform the same act. Because this newly discovered subset of cells seemed to directly reflect acts performed by another in the observer's brain, we named them mirror neurons.

Much as circuits of neurons are believed to store specific memories within the brain, sets of mirror neurons appear to encode templates for specific actions. This property may allow an individual not only to perform basic motor procedures without thinking about them but

Instant Recognition

OUR RESEARCH GROUP was not seeking to support or refute one philosophical position or another when we first noticed mirror neurons. We were studying the brain's motor cortex, particularly an area called F5 associated with hand and mouth movements, to learn how commands to perform certain actions are encoded by the firing patterns of neurons. For this purpose, we were recording the activity of individual neurons in the brains of macaques. Our laboratory contained a rich repertoire of stimuli for the monkeys, and as they performed various actions, such as grasping for a toy or a piece of food, we could see that distinct sets of neurons discharged during the execution of specific motor acts.

in the brain of the act itself, regardless of who was performing it.

Often in biological research, the most direct way to establish the function of a gene, protein or group of cells is simply to eliminate it and then look for deficits in the organism's health or behavior afterward. We could not use this technique to determine the role of mirror neurons, however, because we found them spread across important regions on both sides of the brain, including the premotor and parietal cortices. Destroying the entire mirror neuron system would have produced such broad general cognitive deficits in the monkeys that teasing out specific effects of the missing cells would have been impossible.

So we adopted a different strategy. To test whether mirror neurons play a role in understanding an action rather than just visually registering it, we assessed the neurons' responses when the monkeys could comprehend the meaning of an action without actually seeing it. If mirror neurons truly mediate understanding, we reasoned, their activity should reflect the meaning of the action rather than its visual features. We therefore carried out two series of experiments.

First we tested whether the F5 mirror neurons could "recognize" actions merely from their sounds. We recorded the mirror neurons while a monkey was observing a hand motor act, such as ripping a sheet of paper or breaking a peanut shell, that is accompanied by a distinctive sound. Then we presented the monkey with the sound alone. We found that many F5 mirror neurons that had responded to the visual observation of acts accompanied by sounds also responded to the sounds alone, and we dubbed these cell subsets audiovisual mirror neurons.

Next we theorized that if mirror neurons are truly involved in understanding an action, they should also discharge when the monkey does not actually see the action but has sufficient clues to create a mental representation of it. Thus, we first showed a monkey an experimenter reaching for and grasping a piece of food. Next, a screen was positioned in front of the monkey so that it could not

> *The pattern of activity was a true representation in the brain of the act itself, regardless of who was performing it.*

also to comprehend those acts when they are observed, without any need for explicit reasoning about them. John grasps Mary's action because even as it is happening before his eyes, it is also happening, in effect, inside his head. It is interesting to note that philosophers in the phenomenological tradition long ago posited that one had to experience something within oneself to truly comprehend it. But for neuroscientists, this finding of a physical basis for that idea in the mirror neuron system represents a dramatic change in the way we understand the way we understand.

Then we began to notice something strange: when one of us grasped a piece of food, the monkeys' neurons would fire in the same way as when the monkeys themselves grasped the food. At first we wondered whether this phenomenon could be the result of some trivial factor, such as the monkey performing an unnoticed movement while observing our actions. Once we managed to rule out this possibility and others, including food expectation by the monkeys, we realized that the pattern of neuron activity associated with the observed action was a true representation

Overview/*Meeting of Minds*

- Subsets of neurons in human and monkey brains respond when an individual performs certain actions and also when the subject observes others performing the same movements.
- These "mirror neurons" provide a direct internal experience, and therefore understanding, of another person's act, intention or emotion.
- Mirror neurons may also underlie the ability to imitate another's action, and thereby learn, making the mirror mechanism a bridge between individual brains for communication and connection on multiple levels.

In experiments with monkeys, the authors discovered subsets of neurons in brain-motor areas (*right*) whose activation appeared to represent actions themselves. Firing by these "mirror neurons" could therefore produce in one individual an internal recognition of another's act. Because the neurons' response also reflected comprehension of the movement's goal, the authors concluded that action understanding is a primary purpose of the mirror mechanism. Involvement of the mirror neurons in comprehending the actor's final intention was also seen in their responses, which distinguished between identical grasping actions performed with different intentions.

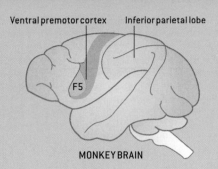

MONKEY BRAIN

UNDERSTANDING ACTION

In early tests, a neuron in the premotor area F5, associated with hand and mouth acts, became highly active when the monkey grasped a raisin on a plate (*1*). The same neuron also responded intensely when an experimenter grasped the raisin as the monkey watched (*2*).

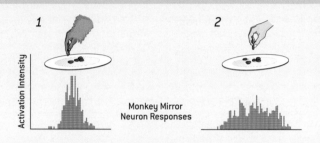

Monkey Mirror Neuron Responses

DISCRIMINATING GOAL

An F5 mirror neuron fired intensely when the monkey observed an experimenter's hand moving to grasp an object (*1*) but not when the hand motioned with no object as its goal (*2*). The same neuron did respond to goal-directed action when the monkey knew an object was behind an opaque screen, although the animal could not see the act's completion (*3*). The neuron responded weakly when the monkey knew no object was behind the screen (*4*).

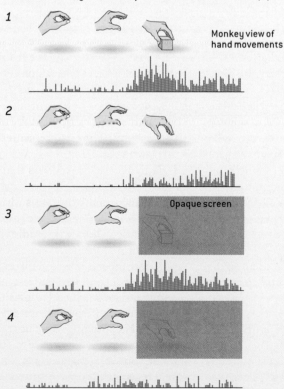

Monkey view of hand movements

Opaque screen

DISCERNING INTENTION

In the inferior parietal lobe, readings from one neuron show intense firing when the monkey grasped a fruit to bring it to its mouth (*1*). The neuron's response was weaker when the monkey grasped the food to place it in a container (*2*). The same mirror neuron also responded intensely when the monkey watched an experimenter perform the grasp-to-eat gesture (*3*) and weakly to the grasp-to-place action (*4*). In all cases, the responses were associated with the grasping act, indicating that the neuron's initial activation encoded an understanding of final intention.

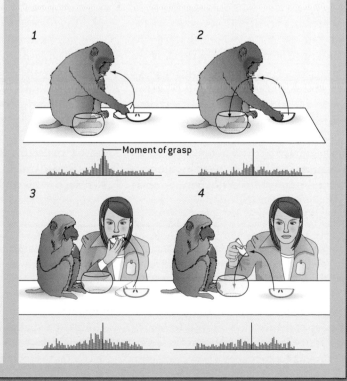

Moment of grasp

Understanding the intentions of others is fundamental to human social behavior, and human mirror neurons appeared to confer that ability in an experiment designed to test their intention recognition. Volunteers were shown film clips (*below left*) depicting two similar cup-grasping actions without context, two contexts without action, and combinations of acts and context that signaled the action's intention: settings for afternoon tea that suggested the cup was being grasped for the purpose of drinking from it or that tea was over and the cup was being cleaned up. Activation of mirror neuron populations in premotor cortex areas in both hemispheres of subjects' brains (*right*) increased most strongly in response to scenes of action with a clear intention. Mirror neurons also distinguished between possible intentions, responding more intensely to the basic biological function of drinking than to the culturally acquired act of cleaning (*below right*).

ACTION

CONTEXT

INTENTION

Premotor cortex

Neuron Activation Intensity

LEFT   RIGHT

ACTION   CONTEXT   INTENTION

Before Tea   Drinking

After Tea   Cleaning Up

Signal Increase

0

Action | Context: Before Tea | Context: After Tea | Intention: Drinking | Intention: Cleaning

---

see the experimenter's hand grasping the food but could only guess the action's conclusion. Nevertheless, more than half the F5 mirror neurons also discharged when the monkey could just imagine what was happening behind the screen.

These experiments confirmed, therefore, that the activity of mirror neurons underpins understanding of motor acts: when comprehension of an action is possible on a nonvisual basis, such as sound or mental representation, mirror neurons do still discharge to signal the act's meaning.

Following these discoveries in the monkey brain, we naturally wondered whether a mirror neuron system also exists in humans. We first obtained strong evidence that it does through a series of experiments that employed various techniques for detecting changes in motor cortex activity. As volunteers ob-

served an experimenter grasping objects or performing meaningless arm gestures, for example, increased neural activation in their hand and arm muscles that would be involved in the same movements suggested a mirror neuron response in the motor areas of their brains. Further investigations using different external measures of cortical activity, such as electroencephalography, also supported the existence of a mirror neuron system in humans. But none of the technologies we had used up to this point allowed us to identify the exact brain areas activated when the volunteers observed motor acts, so we set out to explore this question with direct brain-imaging techniques.

In those experiments, carried out at San Raffaele Hospital in Milan, we used positron-emission tomography (PET) to observe neuronal activity in the brains of

human volunteers as they watched grasping actions performed with different hand grips and then, as a control, looked at stationary objects. In these situations, seeing actions performed by others activated three main areas of the brain's cortex. One of these, the superior temporal sulcus (STS), is known to contain neurons that respond to observations of moving body parts. The other two—the inferior parietal lobule (IPL) and the inferior frontal gyrus (IFG)—correspond, respectively, to the monkey IPL and the monkey ventral premotor cortex, including F5, the areas where we had previously recorded mirror neurons.

These encouraging results suggested a mirror mechanism at work in the human brain as well but still did not fully reveal its scope. If mirror neurons permit an observed act to be directly understood by experiencing it, for example, we wondered to what extent the ultimate goal of the action is also a component of that "understanding."

On Purpose

RETURNING TO our example of John and Mary, we said John knows both that Mary is picking up the flower and that she plans to hand it to him. Her smile gave him a contextual clue to her intention, and in this situation, John's knowledge of Mary's goal is fundamental to his understanding of her action, because giving him the flower is the completion of the movements that make up her act.

When we perform such a gesture ourselves, in reality we are performing a series of linked motor acts whose sequence is determined by our intent: one series of movements picks the flower and brings it to one's own nose to smell, but a partly different set of movements grasps the flower and hands it to someone else. Therefore, our research group set out to explore whether mirror neurons provide an understanding of intention by distinguishing between similar actions with different goals.

For this purpose, we returned to our monkeys to record their parietal neurons under varying conditions. In one set of experiments, a monkey's task was to grasp a piece of food and bring it to its mouth. Next we had the monkey grasp the same item and place it into a container. Interestingly, we found that most of the neurons we recorded discharged differently during the grasping part of the monkey's action, depending on its final goal. This evidence illustrated that the motor system is organized in neuronal chains, each of which encodes the specific intention of the act. We then asked whether this mechanism explains how we understand the intentions of others.

We tested the same grasping neurons for their mirror properties by having a monkey observe an experimenter performing the tasks the monkey itself had done earlier [see box on page 49]. In each instance, most of the mirror neurons were activated differently, depending on whether the experimenter brought the food to his mouth or put it in the container. The patterns of firing in the monkey's brain exactly matched those we observed when the monkey itself performed the acts—mirror neurons that discharged most strongly during grasping-to-eat rather than grasping-to-place did the same when the monkey watched the experimenter perform the corresponding action.

A strict link thus appears to exist between the motor organization of intentional actions and the capacity to understand the intentions of others. When the monkeys observed an action in a particular context, seeing just the first grasping component of the complete movement activated mirror neurons forming a motor chain that also encoded a specific intention. Which chain was activated during their observation of the beginning of an action depended on a variety of factors, such as the nature of the object acted on, the context and the memory of what the observed agent did before.

To see whether a similar mechanism for reading intentions exists in humans, we teamed with Marco Iacoboni and his colleagues at the University of California, Los Angeles, for a functional magnetic resonance imaging (fMRI) experiment on volunteers. Participants in these tests were presented with three kinds of stimuli, all contained within video clips. The first set of images showed a hand grasping a cup against an empty background using two different grips. The second consisted of two scenes containing objects such as plates and cutlery, arranged in one instance as though they were ready for someone to have afternoon tea and in the other as though they were left over from a previously eaten snack and were ready to be cleaned up. The third stimulus set showed a hand grasping a cup in either of those two contexts.

We wanted to establish whether human mirror neurons would distinguish between grasping a cup to drink, as suggested by the ready-for-tea context, and grabbing the cup to take it away, as suggested by the cleanup setting. Our re-

> ### When people use the expression "I feel your pain," they may not realize how literally it could be true.

sults demonstrated not only that they do but also that the mirror neuron system responded strongly to the intention component of an act. Test subjects observing the hand motor acts in the "drinking" or "cleaning" contexts showed differing activation of their mirror neuron systems, and mirror neuron activity was stronger in both those situations than when subjects observed the hand grasping a cup without any context or when looking only at the place settings [see box on opposite page].

Given that humans and monkeys are social species, it is not difficult to see the potential survival advantage of a mechanism, based on mirror neurons, that locks basic motor acts onto a larger motor semantic network, permitting the direct and immediate comprehension of others' behavior without complex cognitive machinery. In social life, however, understanding others' emotions is equal-

THE AUTHORS

GIACOMO RIZZOLATTI, LEONARDO FOGASSI and VITTORIO GALLESE work together at the University of Parma in Italy, where Rizzolatti is director of the neurosciences department and Fogassi and Gallese are associate professors. In the early 1990s their studies of motor systems in the brains of monkeys and humans first revealed the existence of neurons with mirror properties. They have since continued to investigate those mirror neurons in both species as well as the role of the motor system in general cognition. They frequently collaborate with the many other research groups in Europe and the U.S. now also studying the breadth and functions of the mirror neuron system in humans and animals.

ly important. Indeed, emotion is often a key contextual element that signals the intent of an action. That is why we and other research groups have also been exploring whether the mirror system allows us to understand what others feel in addition to what they do.

Connect and Learn

AS WITH ACTIONS, humans undoubtedly understand emotions in more than one way. Observing another person experiencing emotion can trigger a cognitive elaboration of that sensory information, which ultimately results in a logical conclusion about what the other is feeling. It may also, however, result in direct mapping of that sensory information onto the motor structures that would produce the experience of that emotion in the observer. These two means of recognizing emotions are profoundly different: with the first, the observer deduces the emotion but does not feel it; via the second, recognition is firsthand because the mirror mechanism elicits the same emotional state in

the observer. Thus, when people use the expression "I feel your pain" to indicate both comprehension and empathy, they may not realize just how literally true their statement could be.

A paradigmatic example is the emotion of disgust, a basic reaction whose expression has important survival value for fellow members of a species. In its most primitive form, disgust indicates that something the individual tastes or smells is bad and, most likely, dangerous. Once again using fMRI studies, we collaborated with French neuroscientists to show that experiencing disgust as a result of inhaling foul odorants and witnessing disgust on the face of someone else activate the same neural structure—the anterior insula—at some of the very same locations within that structure [see box below]. These results indicate that populations of mirror neurons in the insula become active both when the test participants experience the emotion and when they see it expressed by others. In other words, the observer and the observed share a neural mechanism

that enables a form of direct experiential understanding.

Tania Singer and her colleagues at University College London found similar matches between experienced and observed emotions in the context of pain. In that experiment, the participants felt pain produced by electrodes placed on their hands and then watched electrodes placed on a test partner's hand followed by a cue for painful stimulation. Both situations activated the same regions of the anterior insula and the anterior cingulate cortex in the subjects.

Taken together, such data strongly suggest that humans may comprehend emotions, or at least powerful negative emotions, through a direct mapping mechanism involving parts of the brain that generate visceral motor responses. Such a mirror mechanism for understanding emotions cannot, of course, fully explain all social cognition, but it does provide for the first time a functional neural basis for some of the interpersonal relations on which more complex social behaviors are built. It may be a substrate that allows us to empathize with others, for example. Dysfunction in this mirroring system may also be implicated in empathy deficits, such as those seen in children with autism [see "Broken Mirrors: A Theory of Autism," SCIENTIFIC AMERICAN, November 2006].

Many laboratories, including our own, are continuing to explore these questions, both for their inherent interest and their potential therapeutic applications. If the mirror neuron template of a motor action is partly inscribed in the brain by experience, for instance, then it should theoretically be possible to alleviate motor impairments, such as those suffered following a stroke, by potentiating undamaged action templates. Recent evidence indicates, in fact, that the mirror mechanism also plays a role in the way we initially learn new skills.

Although the word "ape" is often used to denote mimicry, imitation is not an especially well developed ability among nonhuman primates. It is rare in monkeys and limited in the great apes, including chimpanzees and gorillas. For

EMOTIONAL MIRRORS

Feeling disgust activated similar parts of the brain when human volunteers experienced the emotion while smelling a disgusting odor or when the same subjects watched a film clip (*left*) of someone else disgusted. In this brain cross section, neuron populations activated by the experience of disgust are outlined in red, and those activated by seeing disgust are circled in yellow. (Blue outlines the region of investigation, and green indicates areas examined in a previous study.) These overlapping neuron groups may represent a physical neural mechanism for human empathy that permits understanding the emotions of others.

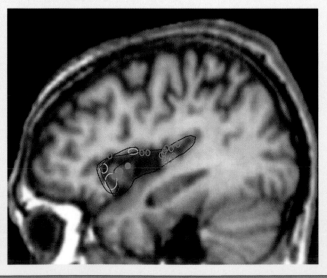

IMITATION requires reproduction of actions performed by another person. If mirror neurons underlie the uniquely human facility for imitation, the mirror system may serve as a bridge that allows us to teach and learn new skills.

humans, in contrast, imitation is a very important means by which we learn and transmit skills, language and culture. Did this advance over our primate relatives evolve on the neural substrate of the mirror neuron system? Iacoboni and his group provided the first evidence that this might be the case when they used fMRI to observe human subjects who were watching and imitating finger movements. Both activities triggered the IFG, part of the mirror neuron system, in particular when the movement had a specific goal.

In all these experiments, however, the movements to be imitated were simple and highly practiced. What role might mirror neurons play when we have to learn completely new and complex motor acts by imitation? To answer this question, Giovanni Buccino at our university and collaborators in Germany recently used fMRI to study participants imitating guitar chords after seeing them played by an expert guitarist. While test subjects observed the expert, their parietofrontal mirror neuron systems became active. And the same area was even more strongly activated during the subjects' imitation of the chord movements. Interestingly, in the interval following observation, while the participants were programming their own imitation of the guitar chords, an additional brain region became active.

Known as prefrontal area 46, this part of the brain is traditionally associated with motor planning and working memory and may therefore play a central role in properly assembling the elementary motor acts that constitute the action the subject is about to imitate.

Many aspects of imitation have long perplexed neuroscientists, including the basic question of how an individual's brain takes in visual information and translates it to be reproduced in motor terms. If the mirror neuron system serves as a bridge in this process, then in addition to providing an understanding of other people's actions, intentions and emotions, it may have evolved to become an important component in the human capacity for observation-based learning of sophisticated cognitive skills.

Scientists do not yet know if the mirror neuron system is unique to primates or if other animals possess it as well. Our own research group is currently testing rats to see if that species also

demonstrates mirror neuron responses. Such internal mirroring may be an ability that developed late in evolution, which would explain why it is more extensive in humans than in monkeys. Because even newborn human and monkey babies can imitate simple gestures such as sticking out the tongue, however, the ability to create mirror templates for observed actions could be innate. And because lack of emotional mirroring ability appears to be a hallmark of autism, we are also working with young autistic children to learn whether they have detectable motor deficits that could signal a general dysfunction of the mirror neuron system.

Only a decade has passed since we published our first discoveries about mirror neurons, and many questions remain to be answered, including the mirror system's possible role in language—one of humanity's most sophisticated cognitive skills. The human mirror neuron system does include Broca's area, a fundamental language-related cortical center. And if, as some linguists believe, human communication first began with facial and hand gestures, then mirror neurons would have played an important role in language evolution. In fact, the mirror mechanism solves two fundamental communication problems: parity and direct comprehension. Parity requires that meaning within the message is the same for the sender as for the recipient. Direct comprehension means that no previous agreement between individuals—on arbitrary symbols, for instance—is needed for them to understand each other. The accord is inherent in the neural organization of both people. Internal mirrors may thus be what allow John and Mary to connect wordlessly and permit human beings in general to communicate on multiple levels. [SA]

MORE TO EXPLORE

Action Recognition in the Premotor Cortex. Vittorio Gallese, Luciano Fadiga, Leonardo Fogassi and Giacomo Rizzolatti in *Brain,* Vol. 119, No. 2, pages 593–609; April 1996.

A Unifying View of the Basis of Social Cognition. V. Gallese, C. Keysers and G. Rizzolatti in *Trends in Cognitive Sciences,* Vol. 8, pages 396–403; 2004.

Grasping the Intentions of Others with One's Own Mirror Neuron System. Marco Iacoboni et al. in *PLoS Biology,* Vol. 3, Issue 3, pages 529–535; March 2005.

Parietal Lobe: From Action Organization to Intention Understanding. Leonardo Fogassi et al. in *Science,* Vol. 302, pages 662–667; April 29, 2005.

Creating False Memories

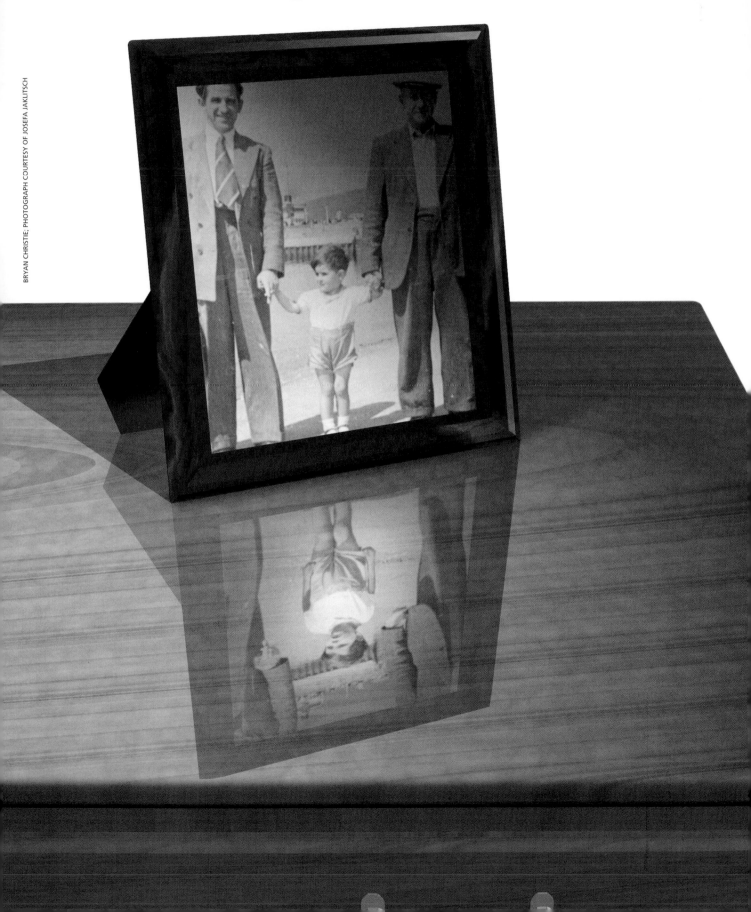

BRYAN CHRISTIE; PHOTOGRAPH COURTESY OF JOSEFA JAKLITSCH

Researchers are showing how suggestion and imagination can create "memories" of events that did not actually occur

by Elizabeth F. Loftus

In 1986 Nadean Cool, a nurse's aide in Wisconsin, sought therapy from a psychiatrist to help her cope with her reaction to a traumatic event experienced by her daughter. During therapy, the psychiatrist used hypnosis and other suggestive techniques to dig out buried memories of abuse that Cool herself had allegedly experienced. In the process, Cool became convinced that she had repressed memories of having been in a satanic cult, of eating babies, of being raped, of having sex with animals and of being forced to watch the murder of her eight-year-old friend. She came to believe that she had more than 120 personalities—children, adults, angels and even a duck—all because, Cool was told, she had experienced severe childhood sexual and physical abuse. The psychiatrist also performed exorcisms on her, one of which lasted for five hours and included the sprinkling of holy water and screams for Satan to leave Cool's body.

When Cool finally realized that false memories had been planted, she sued the psychiatrist for malpractice. In March 1997, after five weeks of trial, her case was settled out of court for $2.4 million.

Nadean Cool is not the only patient to develop false memories as a result of questionable therapy. In Missouri in 1992 a church counselor helped Beth Rutherford to remember during therapy that her father, a clergyman, had regularly raped her between the ages of seven and 14 and that her mother sometimes helped him by holding her down. Under her therapist's guidance, Rutherford developed memories of her father twice impregnating her and forcing her to abort the fetus herself with a coat hanger. The father

had to resign from his post as a clergyman when the allegations were made public. Later medical examination of the daughter revealed, however, that she was still a virgin at age 22 and had never been pregnant. The daughter sued the therapist and received a $1-million settlement in 1996.

About a year earlier two juries returned verdicts against a Minnesota psychiatrist accused of planting false memories by former patients Vynnette Hamanne and Elizabeth Carlson, who under hypnosis and sodium amytal, and after being fed misinformation about the workings of memory, had come to remember horrific abuse by family members. The juries awarded Hammane $2.67 million and Carlson $2.5 million for their ordeals.

In all four cases, the women developed memories about childhood abuse in therapy and then later denied their authenticity. How can we determine if memories of childhood abuse are true or false? Without corroboration, it is very difficult to differentiate between false memories and true ones. Also, in these cases, some memories were contrary to physical evidence, such as explicit and detailed recollections of rape and abortion when medical examination confirmed virginity. How is it possible for people to acquire elaborate and confident false memories? A growing number of investigations demonstrate that under the right circumstances false memories can be instilled rather easily in some people.

My own research into memory distortion goes back to the early 1970s, when I began studies of the "misinformation effect." These studies show that when people who witness an event are later exposed to new and misleading information about it, their recollections often become distorted. In one example, participants viewed a simulated automobile accident at an intersection with

a stop sign. After the viewing, half the participants received a suggestion that the traffic sign was a yield sign. When asked later what traffic sign they remembered seeing at the intersection, those who had been given the suggestion tended to claim that they had seen a yield sign. Those who had not received the phony information were much more accurate in their recollection of the traffic sign.

My students and I have now conducted more than 200 experiments involving over 20,000 individuals that document how exposure to misinformation induces memory distortion. In these studies, people "recalled" a conspicuous barn in a bucolic scene that contained no buildings at all, broken glass and tape recorders that were not in the scenes they viewed, a white instead of a blue vehicle in a crime scene, and Minnie Mouse when they actually saw Mickey Mouse. Taken together, these studies show that misinformation can change an individual's recollection in predictable and sometimes very powerful ways.

Misinformation has the potential for invading our memories when we talk to other people, when we are suggestively interrogated or when we read or view media coverage about some event that we may have experienced ourselves. After more than two decades of exploring the power of misinformation, researchers have learned a great deal about the conditions that make people susceptible to memory modification. Memories are more easily modified, for instance, when the passage of time allows the original memory to fade.

False Childhood Memories

It is one thing to change a detail or two in an otherwise intact memory but quite another to plant a false memory of an event that never happened. To study false memory, my students and I

FALSE MEMORIES are often created by combining actual memories with suggestions received from others. The memory of a happy childhood outing to the beach with father and grandfather, for instance, can be distorted by a suggestion, perhaps from a relative, into a memory of being afraid or lost. False memories also can be induced when a person is encouraged to imagine experiencing specific events without worrying about whether they really happened or not.

first had to find a way to plant a pseudo-memory that would not cause our subjects undue emotional stress, either in the process of creating the false memory or when we revealed that they had been intentionally deceived. Yet we wanted to try to plant a memory that would be at least mildly traumatic, had the experience actually happened.

My research associate, Jacqueline E. Pickrell, and I settled on trying to plant a specific memory of being lost in a shopping mall or large department store at about the age of five. Here's how we did it. We asked our subjects, 24 individuals ranging in age from 18 to 53, to try to remember childhood events that had been recounted to us by a parent, an older sibling or another close relative. We prepared a booklet for each participant containing one-paragraph stories about three events that had actually happened to him or her and one that had not. We constructed the false event using information about a plausible shopping trip provided by a relative, who also verified that the participant had not in fact been lost at about the age of five. The lost-in-the-mall scenario included the following elements: lost for an extended period, crying, aid and comfort by an elderly woman and, finally, reunion with the family.

After reading each story in the book-let, the participants wrote what they remembered about the event. If they did not remember it, they were instructed to write, "I do not remember this." In two follow-up interviews, we told the participants that we were interested in examining how much detail they could remember and how their memories compared with those of their relative. The event paragraphs were not read to them verbatim, but rather parts were provided as retrieval cues. The participants recalled something about 49 of the 72 true events (68 percent) immediately after the initial reading of the booklet and also in each of the two follow-up interviews. After reading the booklet, seven of the 24 participants (29 percent) remembered either partially or fully the false event constructed for them, and in the two follow-up interviews six participants (25 percent) continued to claim that they remembered the fictitious event. Statistically, there were some differences between the true memories and the false ones: participants used more words to describe the true memories, and they rated the true memories as being somewhat more clear. But if an onlooker

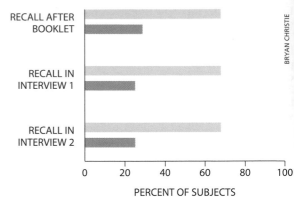

BRYAN CHRISTIE

were to observe many of our participants describe an event, it would be difficult indeed to tell whether the account was of a true or a false memory.

Of course, being lost, however frightening, is not the same as being abused. But the lost-in-the-mall study is not about real experiences of being lost; it is about planting false memories of being lost. The paradigm shows a way of instilling false memories and takes a step toward allowing us to understand how this might happen in real-world settings. Moreover, the study provides evidence that people can be led to remember their past in different ways, and they can

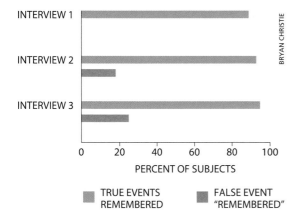

BRYAN CHRISTIE

RECALL OF PLANTED CHILDHOOD EVENTS in this study appears to increase slightly after the details become familiar to the subject and the source of the information is forgotten. Ira Hyman and his colleagues at Western Washington University presented subjects with true events provided by relatives along with a false event—such as spilling a punch bowl on the parents of the bride at a wedding. None of the participants remembered the false event when first told about it, but in two follow-up interviews, initially 18 percent and later 25 percent of the subjects said they remembered something about the incident.

Creating False Memories

FALSE MEMORY TOOK ROOT in roughly 25 percent of the subjects in this study by the author and her co-workers. The study was designed to create a false recollection of being lost at age five on a shopping trip. A booklet prepared for each participant included the false event and three events that he or she had actually experienced. After reading the scenarios, 29 percent of the subjects "recalled" something about being lost in the mall. Follow-up interviews showed there was little variation over time in recalling both the false and true events.

even be coaxed into "remembering" entire events that never happened.

Studies in other laboratories using a similar experimental procedure have produced similar results. For instance, Ira Hyman, Troy H. Husband and F. James Billing of Western Washington University asked college students to recall childhood experiences that had been recounted by their parents. The researchers told the students that the study was about how people remember shared experiences differently. In addition to actual events reported by parents, each participant was given one false event— either an overnight hospitalization for a high fever and a possible ear infection, or a birthday party with pizza and a clown—that supposedly happened at about the age of five. The parents confirmed that neither of these events actually took place.

Hyman found that students fully or partially recalled 84 percent of the true events in the first interview and 88 percent in the second interview. None of the participants recalled the false event during the first interview, but 20 percent said they remembered something about the false event in the second interview. One participant who had been exposed to the emergency hospitalization story later remembered a male doctor, a female nurse and a friend from church who came to visit at the hospital.

In another study, along with true events Hyman presented different false events, such as accidentally spilling a bowl of punch on the parents of the bride at a wedding reception or having to evacuate a grocery store when the overhead sprinkler systems erroneously activated. Again, none of the participants recalled the false event during the first interview, but 18 percent remembered something about it in the second interview and 25 percent in the third interview. For example, during the first interview, one participant, when asked about the fictitious wedding event, stated, "I have no clue. I have never heard that one before." In the second interview, the participant said, "It was an outdoor wedding, and I think we were

running around and knocked something over like the punch bowl or something and made a big mess and of course got yelled at for it."

Imagination Inflation

The finding that an external suggestion can lead to the construction of false childhood memories helps us understand the process by which false memories arise. It is natural to wonder whether this research is applicable in real situations such as being interrogated by law officers or in psychotherapy. Although strong suggestion may not routinely occur in police questioning or therapy, suggestion in the form of an imagination exercise sometimes does. For instance, when trying to obtain a confession, law officers may ask a suspect to imagine having participated in a criminal act. Some mental health professionals encourage patients to imagine childhood events as a way of recovering supposedly hidden memories.

Surveys of clinical psychologists reveal that 11 percent instruct their clients to "let the imagination run wild," and 22 percent tell their clients to "give free rein to the imagination." Therapist Wendy Maltz, author of a popular book on childhood sexual abuse, advocates telling the patient: "Spend time imagin-

ing that you were sexually abused, without worrying about accuracy, proving anything, or having your ideas make sense…. Ask yourself…these questions: What time of day is it? Where are you? Indoors or outdoors? What kind of things are happening? Is there one or more person with you?" Maltz further recommends that therapists continue to ask questions such as "Who would have been likely perpetrators? When were you most vulnerable to sexual abuse in your life?"

The increasing use of such imagination exercises led me and several colleagues to wonder about their consequences. What happens when people imagine childhood experiences that did not happen to them? Does imagining a childhood event increase confidence that it occurred? To explore this, we designed a three-stage procedure. We first asked individuals to indicate the likelihood that certain events happened to them during their childhood. The list contains 40 events, each rated on a scale ranging from "definitely did not happen" to "definitely did happen." Two weeks later we asked the participants to imagine that they had experienced some of these events. Different subjects were asked to imagine different events. Sometime later the participants again were asked to respond to the original list of 40 childhood events, indicating how likely it was that these events actually happened to them.

Consider one of the imagination exercises. Participants are told to imagine playing inside at home after school, hearing a strange noise outside, running toward the window, tripping, falling, reaching out and breaking the window with their hand. In addition, we asked participants questions such as "What did you trip on? How did you feel?"

In one study 24 percent of the participants who imagined the broken-window scenario later reported an increase in confidence that the event had occurred, whereas only 12 percent of those who were not asked to imagine the incident reported an increase in the likelihood that it had taken place. We found this "imagination inflation" effect in each of the eight events that participants were asked to imagine. A number of possible explanations come to mind. An obvious one is that an act of imagination simply makes the event seem more familiar and that familiarity is mistakenly related to childhood memories rather than to the act of imagination. Such source confusion—when a person does not remember the source of information—can be especially acute for the distant experiences of childhood.

Studies by Lyn Goff and Henry L. Roediger III of Washington University of recent rather than childhood experiences more directly connect imagined actions to the construction of false memory. During the initial session, the researchers instructed participants to perform the stated action, imagine doing it or just listen to the statement and do nothing else. The actions were simple ones: knock on the table, lift the stapler, break the toothpick, cross your fingers, roll your eyes. During the second session, the participants were asked to imagine some of the actions that they had not previously performed. During the final session, they answered questions about what actions they actually performed during the initial session. The investigators found that the more times participants imagined an unperformed action, the more likely they were to remember having performed it.

Impossible Memories

It is highly unlikely that an adult can recall genuine episodic memories from the first year of life, in part because the hippocampus, which plays a key role in the creation of memories, has not matured enough to form and store longlasting memories that can be retrieved in adulthood. A procedure for planting "impossible" memories about experiences that occur shortly after birth has been developed by the late Nicholas Spanos and his collaborators at Carleton University. Individuals are led to believe that they have well-coordinated eye movements and visual exploration skills probably because they were born in hospitals that hung swinging, colored mobiles over infant cribs. To confirm whether they had such an experience, half the participants are hypnotized, age-regressed to the day after birth and asked what they remembered. The other half of the group participates in a "guided mnemonic restructuring" procedure that uses age regression as well as active encouragement to re-create the infant experiences by imagining them.

Spanos and his co-workers found that the vast majority of their subjects were susceptible to these memory-planting procedures. Both the hypnotic and guided participants reported infant memories. Surprisingly, the guided group did so somewhat more (95 versus 70 percent). Both groups remembered the colored mobile at a relatively high rate (56 percent of the guided group and 46 percent of the hypnotic subjects). Many participants who did not remember the

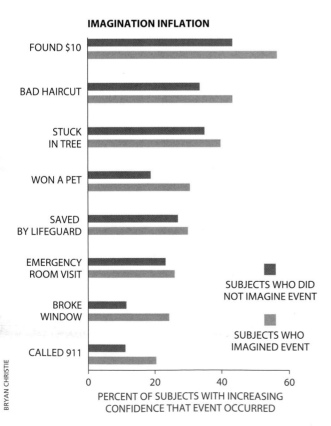

IMAGINATION INFLATION

FOUND $10
BAD HAIRCUT
STUCK IN TREE
WON A PET
SAVED BY LIFEGUARD
EMERGENCY ROOM VISIT
BROKE WINDOW
CALLED 911

0   20   40   60
PERCENT OF SUBJECTS WITH INCREASING CONFIDENCE THAT EVENT OCCURRED

■ SUBJECTS WHO DID NOT IMAGINE EVENT
■ SUBJECTS WHO IMAGINED EVENT

BRYAN CHRISTIE

IMAGINING AN EVENT can increase a person's belief that the fictitious event actually happened. To study the "imagination inflation" effect, the author and her colleagues asked participants to indicate on a scale the likelihood that each of 40 events occurred during their childhood. Two weeks later they were given guidance in imagining some of the events they said had not taken place and then were asked to rate the original 40 events again. Whereas all participants showed increased confidence that the events had occurred, those who took part in actively imagining the events reported an even greater increase.

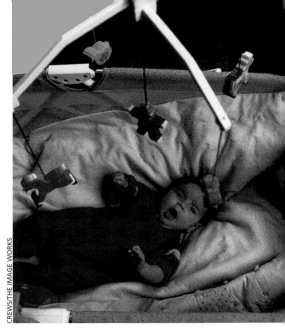

MEMORIES OF INFANCY—such as a mobile hanging over a crib—can be induced even though it is highly unlikely that events from the first year of life can be recalled. In a study by the late Nicholas Spanos and his colleagues at Carleton University, "impossible" memories of the first day of life were planted using either hypnosis or a guided mnemonic restructuring procedure. The mobile was "remembered" by 46 percent of the hypnotized group and by 56 percent of the guided group.

mobile did recall other things, such as doctors, nurses, bright lights, cribs and masks. Also, in both groups, of those who reported memories of infancy, 49 percent felt that they were real memories, as opposed to 16 percent who claimed that they were merely fantasies. These findings confirm earlier studies that many individuals can be led to construct complex, vivid and detailed false memories via a rather simple procedure. Hypnosis clearly is not necessary.

How False Memories Form

In the lost-in-the-mall study, implantation of false memory occurred when another person, usually a family member, claimed that the incident happened. Corroboration of an event by another person can be a powerful technique for instilling a false memory. In fact, merely claiming to have seen a person do something can lead that person to make a false confession of wrongdoing.

This effect was demonstrated in a study by Saul M. Kassin and his colleagues at Williams College, who investigated the reactions of individuals falsely accused of damaging a computer by pressing the wrong key. The innocent participants initially denied the charge, but when a confederate said that she had seen them perform the action, many participants signed a confession, internalized guilt for the act and went on to confabulate details that were consistent with that belief. These findings show that false

incriminating evidence can induce people to accept guilt for a crime they did not commit and even to develop memories to support their guilty feelings.

Research is beginning to give us an understanding of how false memories of complete, emotional and self-participatory experiences are created in adults. First, there are social demands on individuals to remember; for instance, researchers exert some pressure on participants in a study to come up with memories. Second, memory construction by imagining events can be explicitly encouraged when people are having trouble remembering. And, finally, individuals can be encouraged not to think about whether their constructions are real or not. Creation of false memories is most likely to occur when these external factors are present, whether in an experimental setting, in a therapeutic setting or during everyday activities.

False memories are constructed by combining actual memories with the content of suggestions received from others. During the process, individuals may forget the source of the information. This is a classic example of source confusion, in which the content and the source become dissociated.

Of course, because we can implant false childhood memories in some individuals in no way implies that all memories that arise after suggestion are necessarily false. Put another way, although experimental work on the creation of false memories may raise doubt about

the validity of long-buried memories, such as repeated trauma, it in no way disproves them. Without corroboration, there is little that can be done to help even the most experienced evaluator to differentiate true memories from ones that were suggestively planted.

The precise mechanisms by which such false memories are constructed await further research. We still have much to learn about the degree of confidence and the characteristics of false memories created in these ways, and we need to discover what types of individuals are particularly susceptible to these forms of suggestion and who is resistant.

As we continue this work, it is important to heed the cautionary tale in the data we have already obtained: mental health professionals and others must be aware of how greatly they can influence the recollection of events and of the urgent need for maintaining restraint in situations in which imagination is used as an aid in recovering presumably lost memories. [SA]

The Author

ELIZABETH F. LOFTUS is professor of psychology and adjunct professor of law at the University of Washington. She received her Ph.D. in psychology from Stanford University in 1970. Her research has focused on human memory, eyewitness testimony and courtroom procedure. Loftus has published 18 books and more than 250 scientific articles and has served as an expert witness or consultant in hundreds of trials, including the McMartin preschool molestation case. Her book *Eyewitness Testimony* won a National Media Award from the American Psychological Foundation. She has received honorary doctorates from Miami University, Leiden University and John Jay College of Criminal Justice. Loftus was recently elected president of the American Psychological Society.

Further Reading

THE MYTH OF REPRESSED MEMORY. Elizabeth F. Loftus and Katherine Ketcham. St. Martin's Press, 1994.
THE SOCIAL PSYCHOLOGY OF FALSE CONFESSIONS: COMPLIANCE, INTERNALIZATION, AND CONFABULATION. Saul M. Kassin and Katherine L. Kiechel in *Psychological Science,* Vol. 7, No. 3, pages 125–128; May 1996.
IMAGINATION INFLATION: IMAGINING A CHILDHOOD EVENT INFLATES CONFIDENCE THAT IT OCCURRED. Maryanne Garry, Charles G. Manning, Elizabeth F. Loftus and Steven J. Sherman in *Psychonomic Bulletin and Review,* Vol. 3, No. 2, pages 208–214; June 1996.
REMEMBERING OUR PAST: STUDIES IN AUTOBIOGRAPHICAL MEMORY. Edited by David C. Rubin. Cambridge University Press, 1996.
SEARCHING FOR MEMORY: THE BRAIN, THE MIND, AND THE PAST. Daniel L. Schacter. BasicBooks, 1996.

Talking about Terrorism

HOW WE CHARACTERIZE AN ISSUE AFFECTS HOW WE THINK ABOUT IT. REPLACING THE "WAR ON TERROR" METAPHOR WITH OTHER WAYS OF FRAMING COUNTERTERRORISM MIGHT HELP US CURTAIL THE VIOLENCE MORE EFFECTIVELY

BY ARIE W. KRUGLANSKI, MARTHA CRENSHAW, JERROLD M. POST AND JEFF VICTOROFF

On the eve of our national election, we realize that one challenging issue facing the next president is how to address terrorism and the options for counterterrorism. As psychological research has made clear, what he and his administration say about these issues will influence how the public thinks about them—and will affect our national and international policy. [For more on the power of words, see "When Words Decide," by Barry Schwartz; SCIENTIFIC AMERICAN MIND, August/September 2007.]

Since the attacks on the World Trade Center and the Pentagon in 2001, the Bush administration has used a battle metaphor: the "global war on terrorism" and the "war on terror." Such descriptive terms simplify complex realities, making them more mentally manageable. But they do not adequately represent the complexities of the problem, resulting in selective perception of the facts, and they may reflect the views of only a few key policy makers. Nevertheless, they can guide national decision making. The wars that began in Afghanistan in 2001 and Iraq in 2003 clearly demonstrate that the concept of a war to combat a method of violence used by nonstate agents is more than rhetoric.

Although the war metaphor has some advantages, the next president should consider other terms that lead to thinking that is more nuanced—and ultimately more effective. Viewing counterterrorism through the lens of law enforcement, for example, may yield more tightly focused tactics that are less likely to provoke resentment and backlash and are also less costly than war. Two other metaphors—relating counterterrorism to disease containment or prejudice reduction—home in on many of the deeply rooted psychological underpinnings of terrorism and, in doing so, suggest strategies that may chip away at the motivations of terrorists and thus may be the most successful at squelching the scourge in the long run [see "Inside the Terrorist Mind," by Annette Schaefer; SCIENTIFIC AMERICAN MIND, December 2007/January 2008].

Declaring War

The Bush administration's framing of terrorism as an act of war is a departure from past administrations' ways of thinking. Presidents Richard M. Nixon and Ronald Reagan, for example, preferred a disease metaphor. President Bill Clinton's general themes were the pursuit of justice, law enforcement and international cooperation. Clinton wanted to deny "victory" to terrorists, but he and other previous presidents stopped short of the word "war."

President George W. Bush adopted the war construct immediately. On the morning of September 12, 2001, after a meeting of the National Security Council, the president told reporters: "The deliberate and deadly attacks which were carried out yesterday against our country were more than acts of terror. They were acts of war."

The war metaphor helps to define the American perception of the threat of terrorism. If terrorism is war, then the national security, indeed the existence, of each side is threatened. The conflict is zero-sum; the outcome will be victory for one side or the other. Being in a state of war also requires national unity, and dissent is easily interpreted as unpatriotic. The solution has to be military. Thus, the Department of Defense must play a lead role in shaping policy, and the president's duties as commander in chief must take precedence over his other tasks. An expansion of executive power accompanies the war metaphor: measures that would not be acceptable in peacetime, such as restrictions on civil liberties and brutal interrogation practices, are now considered essential.

But in several ways, the struggle against terrorism differs significantly from conventional war. First, the entity that attacked the U.S. in 2001 was not a state. It was an organization, al Qaeda, with a territorial base within a weak "failed state," Afghanistan, whose ruling Taliban regime was not internationally recognized. Since 2001 the entity that the U.S. is fighting has become even more amorphous and less like a state. It has progressed from the so-called terrorist organizations to an ideology that aspires to world domination. David Brooks, writing in the *New York Times* on September 21, 2006 , called it "chaos theory in human form—an ever-shifting array of state and nonstate actors who cooperate, coagulate, divide, feud and feed on one another without end."

Victory in a war on terrorism is similarly difficult to define. A typical war ends in the capitulation of the enemy, but al Qaeda is unlikely to surrender formally. In 2006 the revised (2002) U.S. National Security Strategy, articulated in a White House "wartime" document, set a goal "to defeat global terrorism." It will be difficult to tell when this objective, which involves eradicating a method of violence and a way of thinking, has been met. As a result, the war drags on, breeding disappointment with the results and a public outcry to bring the troops home.

The psychological rationale of war is to bring the enemy

President George W. Bush raises an American flag at the site of the World Trade Center on September 14, 2001. Two days earlier he had described the deadly attacks as "acts of war."

to its knees and to convince it and its support base that terrorism is counterproductive. And yet experience in Chechnya, Afghanistan, Iraq, Ireland, and the West Bank and Gaza Strip suggests that the use of military force does little to "prove" the inefficacy of terrorism. Military strikes against terrorist targets may temporarily interfere with terrorists' ability to launch their operations, but they do not generally lessen the motivation to engage in violence—and may even boost it as a result of the enmity that foreign occupation typically engenders and of the injustice and excesses of war.

The war concept also deafens ears to the underlying troubles of the terrorists—the frustrations and grievances that may have fostered terrorism, as well as the belief systems that lent it ideological sustenance. Meanwhile the metaphor encourages stereotyping and discrimination against members of the broad social categories to which terrorists may belong, such as Muslims, Saudi Arabians or Middle Easterners.

Finally, framing counterterrorism as war has considerable costs. It threatens to corrupt society's values, disrupt its orderly functioning and reshuffle its priorities. War calls for the disproportionate investment of a nation's resources, with correspondingly less left for other concerns, including the economy, health care and education. "Collateral damage," ethnic profiling, harsh interrogation tactics and unlimited internment of suspects may all be condoned in the name of security and excused by the uniqueness of circumstances the war concept implies. These costs are especially steep in a war that has no definite end.

Fighting Crime

Whereas war is a reaction to a massive confrontation, law enforcement generally follows more restricted challenges—akin in many ways to those typically presented by terrorism. For instance, extensive police work, a trial and convictions followed the 1993 truck bombing in the World Trade Center parking garage that resulted in six deaths, hundreds of injuries and property damage just under half a billion dollars. In contrast, war was the response to the 3,000 deaths and tens of billions of dollars in damage from the 9/11 attacks.

A U.S. captain interrogates an Iraqi suspected of taking part in a roadside attack on Americans.

In support of the law-enforcement approach, Senator John Kerry of Massachusetts stated in a presidential candidates' debate in South Carolina in 2004 that although counterterrorism will be "occasionally military," it should be "primarily an intelligence and law-enforcement operation that requires cooperation around the world." The United Nations has never been able to agree on a definition of terrorism but has developed articles prohibiting acts such as airline hijacking and violence against diplomatic persons, consistent with a law-enforcement metaphor. After all, terrorists often engage in crime as conventionally defined, and suspected terrorists in the U.S. are typically prosecuted for criminal offenses rather than terrorism—commonly racketeering, possession of firearms and conspiracy.

FAST FACTS
Mind Your Metaphor

1 ›› Since the attacks on September 11, 2001, the Bush administration has used a war metaphor to define counterterrorism strategy. Such a description may simplify a complex reality, making it more mentally manageable, but it may also oversimplify and distort reality.

2 ›› Metaphors can guide national decision making. The wars that began in Afghanistan in 2001 and Iraq in 2003 clearly demonstrate that the concept of a war to combat a method of violence used by nonstate agents is more than rhetoric.

3 ›› Viewing counterterrorism through the lens of law enforcement may yield more tightly focused tactics that are less costly than war and less likely to provoke resentment and backlash.

4 ›› Relating counterterrorism to disease containment or prejudice reduction shifts the focus to the psychological underpinnings of terrorism and, in doing so, may suggest successful long-term strategies that chip away at the motivations of terrorists.

One advantage of the law-enforcement metaphor over the war concept is its focus on the particular perpetrators in violation of the legal code rather than on an actor vaguely defined as the "enemy." Such an emphasis is less likely to incite discrimination against entire groups of people. And as an ongoing concern, law enforcement does not suggest the need for an overwhelming financial commitment but rather must compete for resources with education, jobs, housing and welfare.

The law-enforcement idea also limits the costs of mistakes. Civilian casualties, nearly unavoidable in bombing raids of terrorist targets under the war metaphor, are unlikely with law-enforcement policies, which are thus less apt to fuel anger toward the West and thereby boost support for terrorist organizations. What is more, the experience of the Israelis and the British suggests that successful counterterrorism often resembles painstaking police work more than it does war. That is, effective police work requires understanding a local culture and geography, developing local relationships and cultivating local sources of information—efforts for which an army is ill prepared.

International cooperation in counterterrorism is also more possible under the law-enforcement approach. Whereas the international community is basically in favor of law and order, the war metaphor is often too demanding for many states to embrace. For example, although France strongly opposed the Iraq War, American and French law enforcement have cooperated very effectively since 9/11.

And yet terrorism, unlike most crimes, is ideologically inspired. In contrast to typical criminals, who tend to have selfish, personal motivations, terrorists are often trying to change the world and frequently believe they are serving a cause that will achieve a greater good. Because of such grand ideas, terrorists often inspire admiration and respect in their communities. During much of the second Intifada, which began in September 2000 and ended this past June, public opinion polls conducted among Palestinians revealed that about 80 percent supported suicide attacks against Israelis. In such situations, law-enforcement officials may have difficulty convincing the public to help them fight crimes related to terrorism.

Finally, because law-enforcement tactics do not generally dampen the motivation to engage in terrorism, their success in thwarting attacks is often short-lived. Terrorists are a determined and inventive bunch, and sooner or later they are likely to find other means of carrying out their plans, for instance, resorting to suicide missions if necessary.

Containing an Epidemic

The social epidemic metaphor for counterterrorism likens the spread of terrorist ideas to the transmission of infectious disease: an external agent such as a pathogen or violent way of thinking infects a susceptible host—a nonimmune or psychologically vulnerable population—in an environment that brings them together. In that environment a vector—such as the malaria-carrying *Anopheles* mosquito or the Internet—facilitates the transmission of a pathogen or ideas.

The disease metaphor of terrorism guides intelligible questions as to the origins of an outbreak, its boundaries, social contours and method of

Extensive police work—not war—followed the 1993 truck bombing in the World Trade Center parking garage. The bombing left six dead and hundreds injured.

Officials destroy thousands of confiscated firearms in Brazil. In the U.S., suspected terrorists are commonly prosecuted for illegal possession of firearms.

RENZO GOSTOLI AP Photo

transmission, along with who is most at risk of "infection." It casts terrorism, like disease, as an outgrowth of a complex interaction among people, pathogens and the environment. It thus suggests that rolling back terrorism requires a multipronged effort to tackle each of these elements just as controlling malaria requires preventive methods that target its environmental contributors, such as spraying the ponds in which the mosquitoes breed and supplying people with protective clothing and mosquito nets.

This metaphor offers a lens through which to more closely examine the underlying psychological forces behind terrorism. The agent or pathogen in this case is a terrorism-justifying ideology that includes a collective grievance, such as humiliation of one's nation or religious group, a culprit or party responsible for the grievance, and a belief that terrorism is a morally justifiable and effective tool for redressing the grievance. A hate-monger-

ing leader typically helps to promote a potent "us versus them" social psychology, setting in motion powerful group dynamics centered on the ideology.

A terrorist philosophy may be propagated by any of several vectors or vehicles, one of the most prominent being the mosque, where young Muslims are inculcated with an unquestioning reverence for Allah. The Middle Eastern prisoners whom a team of psychologists led by one of us (Post) interviewed in 2002 consistently cited the mosque as the place where most members were initially introduced to the Palestinian cause.

The Internet may also facilitate spread of the ideological pathogen. In 2007 Army Brigadier General John Custer, head of intelligence at central command, responsible for Iraq and Afghanistan, stated on *CBS News:* "Without doubt, the Internet is the single most important venue for the radicalization of Islamic youth." Experts estimate that 5,000 jihad sites are currently in operation. In one recruitment drive, potential converts are bombarded with religious decrees and anti-American propaganda, provided with manuals on how to be a terrorist and—as they are led through a maze of secret chat rooms—given instructions on how to make the journey to Iraq to fight U.S. and coalition forces there.

The Internet is thus one obvious target for counterterrorism. In the Saudi Al-Sakinah ("Tranquility") campaign, Muslim legal scholars and propagators of Islam—assisted by psychologists and sociologists—enter extremist Web sites and forums and converse with the participants to bring them to renounce their extremist ideas. The campaign's organizers believe these efforts have been successful in many cases (although that claim needs to be more rigorously examined).

In addition to these vehicles, the propagation of terrorism requires a receptive population. Such susceptibility can arise from early socialization to a terrorism-justifying

(The Authors)

ARIE W. KRUGLANSKI is Distinguished University Professor in Psychology at the University of Maryland and co-director of START (National Consortium for the Study of Terrorism and Responses to Terrorism). MARTHA CRENSHAW is professor of political science and senior fellow at the Center for International Security and Cooperation at Stanford University. JERROLD M. POST is professor of psychiatry, political psychology and international affairs at George Washington University. JEFF VICTOROFF is associate professor of clinical neurology and psychiatry at the University of Southern California, specializing in human aggression and the psychology of terrorists.

ideology and personal circumstances that render the ideology appealing. Inculcation at an early age can build hatred into a child. In one campaign, the Hezbollah Shiite youth movement "Imam al-Mahdi Scouts," tens of thousands of children aged eight to 16 are indoctrinated with the ideology of radical Iranian Islam, whereas kindergarteners are a target audience for the educational efforts of Hamas.

Personal suffering and frustrations can add to the vulnerability. For people growing up or currently living in

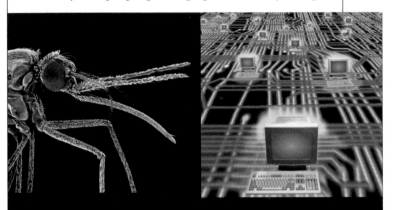

Just as the *Anopheles* mosquito transmits the malaria pathogen, the Internet can facilitate the spread of terrorist ideology.

repressed or limited socioeconomic conditions, academic or economic achievement may seem remote. Thus, many people seek success instead as fighters for a terrorist cause. Traumatic experiences such as having a relative or friend killed by the enemy may increase the desire to embrace collectivistic causes. Creating alternative paths to success might immunize a susceptible population by enabling bright, educated individuals to thrive within their culture rather than striking out in despair.

Stemming Prejudice

Rather than approaching terrorism as a problem perpetuated by the terrorists alone, as the other three metaphors do, the metaphor of prejudice reduction shifts the focus from a unilateral to a bilateral concern and casts terrorism as one expression of tense and deteriorating intergroup relations. A poignant example of such incendiary associations involves Muslim immigrants in Europe and the ethnically native European populations. Three of the

▶▶ **More Science**
See the *Psychological Science in the Public Interest* article, "What Should This Fight Be Called? Metaphors of Counterterrorism and Their Implications," on which this story is based at the Association for Psychological Science's Web site: **www.psychologicalscience.org**

terrorist pilots in the September 11 attacks—Mohamed Atta, Marwan al-Shehhi and Ziad Jarrah—were young Muslims who spent extended periods living in Europe. Since then, a series of attacks, interrupted attacks and plots has been linked to other young Muslims with European background. Most recently, eight Muslim doctors or doctors in training working in British hospitals were arrested in connection with two attempts to explode car bombs in downtown London on June 29, 2007, and an attempt the next day to ram a flaming Jeep into the main entrance of the Glasgow airport.

According to a 2006 report by the Pew Global Attitudes Project, 58 to 70 percent of both Muslims and non-Muslims in Great Britain, France and Germany say that intergroup relations are bad. Cultural differences may explain part of the problem. For instance, many non-Muslim Europeans tend to hold that Muslims are fanatical, violent and disrespectful of women, and most are very or somewhat concerned about the rise of Islamic extremism in their country. As a result of such attitudes, Muslims may be discriminated against in housing, employment and services. Muslim and non-Muslim Europeans also tend not to visit the same stores or entertainment and sporting venues, extending the separation of the two cultures to everyday life.

Although such tensions may not constitute sufficient conditions for terrorism, they may instill the readiness to buy into a terrorism-justifying ideology and are potential harbingers of violent intergroup conflict. For example, 24 percent of British Muslims and 35 percent of French Muslims endorse the statement that violence against civilian targets is sometimes or rarely justified in the service of Islam, according to the Pew report.

Multiple initiatives are under way to enhance integration and reduce friction between Muslims and non-Muslims in Europe. Some of them involve efforts to document discriminatory behavior or civil-rights violations; others strive to promote dialogue or involve legislation to punish discriminatory behaviors in employment, housing and banking.

Despite such efforts, social scientists have done little to evaluate what works to enhance social integration and eliminate tensions. And yet prejudice and discrimination have been among the most intensively studied social psychological phenomena. In particular, a wealth of experimental research has shown that creating opportunities for two groups to meet and interact with each other under agreeable circumstances can go a long way toward reducing prejudice. In the so-called contact hypothesis described by Harvard University psychologist Gordon Allport in his

1954 text *The Nature of Prejudice,* the key is interaction or contact between equal-status members of each group in the pursuit of common goals.

In 2006 psychologists Thomas F. Pettigrew of the University of California, Santa Cruz, and Linda R. Tropp of Boston College reported in a meta-analysis of 515 studies, which included 713 population samples and 1,383 tests, that rates of prejudice fall significantly with contact. Some types of interventions appear to work better than others do: although incidental contact or travel excursions seem to yield little benefit, residential interaction does help; educational and work-based contact is even more valuable, and the best effects were seen in recreational contexts. And, as Allport had argued, when authorities sanction the meetings, that fact predicts success better than any other factor.

Media or community portrayals of aggressive, humiliating or discriminatory activities perpetrated by one group against the other, however, may undermine contact in isolated settings. Efforts at prejudice reduction should include media campaigns and enforcement of antidiscrimination policies as well as immigration laws, educational programs and foreign policy initiatives designed to augment the good will generated by contact programs. And because prejudice is strongly related to real economic disparities and is augmented by a sense of injustice, psychological efforts may work best if combined with credible policies aimed at the elimination of objective inequalities.

Alliances

Prejudicial attitudes are by no means the only explanation for aggression that may translate to terrorism. What is more, the contact prescription that accompanies the idea of prejudice reduction emphasizes cooperative secular activities, thereby failing to address the radical religious notions that fuel terrorism. More generally, the concept of prejudice reduction, like the epidemic metaphor, neglects the short-term challenges posed by terrorism, including the need to counter specific terrorist schemes and protect societies from the immediate threats these entail.

Thus, no single metaphor can fully encapsulate counterterrorism. Each beams a searchlight on specific psychological pieces of the puzzle, illuminating some of its aspects while leaving others in darkness. Jointly, however, these four descriptions manage to convey the considerable complexity behind the violent acts that counterterrorism policies are designed to thwart.

To achieve this broader perspective, we recommend a comprehensive approach involving collaboration between military and law-enforcement experts, along with social scientists who can highlight the likely psychological, po-

As one sign of strained—and potentially incendiary—relations, Muslim and non-Muslim Europeans tend to visit separate stores. This Beurger King Muslim caters to Islamic clientele.

litical or sociological ramifications of various counterterrorism initiatives. Admittedly, setting up such an alliance may not be easy, and long-term considerations may seem at odds with, or tangential to, current security needs.

Nevertheless, academics are finding their way into the relevant security circles. The Homeland Security Act of 2002 established the University Programs initiative, which has led to centers of excellence at U.S. universities that study the social and behavioral (among other) aspects of terrorism. This law has provided a conduit between academic research in the behavioral and social sciences and a government national security agency. In the future, we hope that new cadres of security experts who have been educated in the group and psychological facets of terrorism will lead the U.S. toward more sophisticated and highly effective counterterrorism strategies. **M**

(Further Reading)

◆ **The Mind of the Terrorist: A Review and Critique of Psychological Approaches.** J. Victoroff in *Journal of Conflict Resolution,* Vol. 49, No. 1, pages 3–42; February 2005.

◆ **When Hatred Is Bred in the Bone: Psycho-Cultural Foundations of Contemporary Terrorism.** J. M. Post in *Political Psychology,* Vol. 26, No. 4, pages 615–636; August 2005.

◆ **The Psychology of Terrorism: "Syndrome" versus "Tool" Perspectives.** A. W. Kruglanski and S. Fishman in *Terrorism and Political Violence,* Vol. 18, No. 2, pages 193–215; 2006.

◆ **Explaining Suicide Terrorism: A Review Essay.** M. Crenshaw in *Security Studies,* Vol. 16, No. 1, pages 133–162; January 2007.

◆ **War versus Justice in Response to Terrorist Attacks: Competing Frames and Their Implications.** C. McCauley in *Psychology of Terrorism.* Edited by B. Bongar, L. M. Brown, L. E. Beutler, J. N. Breckenridge and P. G. Zimbardo. Oxford University Press, 2007.

The Secret to Raising Smart Kids

Hint: Don't tell your kids that they are. More than three decades of research shows that a focus on effort—not on intelligence or ability—is key to success in school and in life

By Carol S. Dweck

A brilliant student, Jonathan sailed through grade school. He completed his assignments easily and routinely earned As. Jonathan puzzled over why some of his classmates struggled, and his parents told him he had a special gift. In the seventh grade, however, Jonathan suddenly lost interest in school, refusing to do homework or study for tests. As a consequence, his grades plummeted. His parents tried to boost their son's confidence by assuring him that he was very smart. But their attempts failed to motivate Jonathan (who is a composite drawn from several children). Schoolwork, their son maintained, was boring and pointless.

Our society worships talent, and many people assume that possessing superior intel-

Young people who believe that their intelligence alone will enable them to succeed in school are often discouraged when the going gets tough.

ligence or ability—along with confidence in that ability—is a recipe for success. In fact, however, more than 30 years of scientific investigation suggests that an overemphasis on intellect or talent leaves people vulnerable to failure, fearful of challenges and unwilling to remedy their shortcomings.

The result plays out in children like Jonathan, who coast through the early grades under the dangerous notion that no-effort academic achievement defines them as smart or gifted. Such children hold an implicit belief that intelligence is innate and fixed, making striving to learn seem far less important than being (or looking) smart. This belief also makes them see challenges, mistakes and even the need to exert effort as threats to their ego rather than as opportunities to improve. And it causes them to lose confidence and motivation when the work is no longer easy for them.

Praising children's innate abilities, as Jonathan's parents did, reinforces this mind-set, which can also prevent young athletes or people in the workforce and even marriages from living up to their potential. On the other hand, our studies show that teaching people to have a "growth mind-set," which encourages a focus on effort rather than on intelligence or talent, helps make them into high achievers in school and in life.

The Opportunity of Defeat

I first began to investigate the underpinnings of human motivation—and how people persevere after setbacks—as a psychology graduate student at Yale University in the 1960s. Animal experiments by psychologists Martin Seligman, Steven Maier and Richard Solomon of the University of Pennsylvania had shown that after repeated failures, most animals conclude that a situation is hopeless and beyond their control. After such an experience, the researchers found, an animal often remains passive even when it can affect change—a state they called learned helplessness.

People can learn to be helpless, too, but not everyone reacts to setbacks this way. I wondered:

FAST FACTS
Growing Pains

1》 Many people assume that superior intelligence or ability is a key to success. But more than three decades of research shows that an overemphasis on intellect or talent— and the implication that such traits are innate and fixed—leaves people vulnerable to failure, fearful of challenges and unmotivated to learn.

2》 Teaching people to have a "growth mind-set," which encourages a focus on effort rather than on intelligence or talent, produces high achievers in school and in life.

3》 Parents and teachers can engender a growth mind-set in children by praising them for their effort or persistence (rather than for their intelligence), by telling success stories that emphasize hard work and love of learning, and by teaching them about the brain as a learning machine.

Why do some students give up when they encounter difficulty, whereas others who are no more skilled continue to strive and learn? One answer, I soon discovered, lay in people's beliefs about *why* they had failed.

In particular, attributing poor performance to a lack of ability depresses motivation more than does the belief that lack of effort is to blame. In 1972, when I taught a group of elementary and middle school children who displayed helpless behavior in school that a lack of effort (rather than lack of ability) led to their mistakes on math problems, the kids learned to keep trying when the problems got tough. They also solved many of the problems even in the face of difficulty. Another group of helpless children who were simply rewarded for their success on easy problems did not improve their ability to solve hard math problems. These experiments were an early indication that a focus on effort can help resolve helplessness and engender success.

Subsequent studies revealed that the most persistent students do not ruminate about their own failure much at all but instead think of mistakes as problems to be solved. At the University of Illinois in the 1970s I, along with my then graduate student Carol Diener, asked 60 fifth graders to think out loud while they solved very difficult pattern-recognition problems. Some students reacted defensively to mistakes, denigrating their skills with comments such as "I never did have a good rememory," and their problem-solving strategies deteriorated.

Others, meanwhile, focused on fixing errors and honing their skills. One advised himself: "I should slow down and try to figure this out." Two schoolchildren were particularly inspiring. One, in the wake of difficulty, pulled up his chair, rubbed his hands together, smacked his lips and said, "I love a challenge!" The other, also confronting the hard problems, looked up at the experimenter and approvingly declared, "I was *hoping* this would be informative!" Predictably, the students with this attitude outperformed their cohorts in these studies.

Two Views of Intelligence

Several years later I developed a broader theory of what separates the two general classes of learners—helpless versus mastery-oriented. I re-alized that these different types of students not only explain their failures differently, but they also hold different "theories" of intelligence. The helpless ones believe that intelligence is a fixed trait: you have only a certain amount, and that's that. I call this a "fixed mind-set." Mistakes crack their self-confidence because they attribute errors to a lack of ability, which they feel powerless to change. They avoid challenges because challenges make mistakes more likely and looking smart less so. Like Jonathan, such children shun effort in the belief that having to work hard means they are dumb.

The mastery-oriented children, on the other hand, think intelligence is malleable and can be developed through education and hard work. They want to learn above all else. After all, if you believe that you can expand your intellectual skills, you want to do just that. Because slipups stem from a lack of effort, not ability, they can be remedied by more effort. Challenges are energizing rather than intimidating; they offer opportunities to learn. Students with such a growth

Mind-set and Math Grades

Students who believed that intelligence is malleable (*growth mind-set line*) earned higher math grades in the fall of seventh grade than those who believed in static intelligence (*fixed mind-set line*), even though the two groups had equivalent math achievement test scores in the sixth grade. The grades of the growth mind-set group then improved over the next two years, whereas the grades of the fixed mind-set students declined.

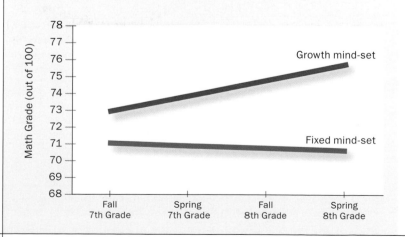

BY L. S. BLACKWELL, K. H. TRZESNIEWSKI AND C. S. DWECK, IN *CHILD DEVELOPMENT*, VOL. 78, NO. 1; JANUARY/FEBRUARY 2007

A for Effort

According to a survey we conducted in the mid-1990s, 85 percent of parents believed that praising children's ability or intelligence when they perform well is important for making them feel smart. But our work shows that praising a child's intelligence makes a child fragile and defensive. So, too, does generic praise that suggests a stable trait, such as "You are a good artist." Praise is very valuable, however, if it is carefully worded. Praise for the specific process a child used to accomplish something fosters motivation and confidence by focusing children on the actions that lead to success. Such process praise may involve commending effort, strategies, focus, persistence in the face of difficulty, and willingness to take on challenges. Here are some examples:

- You did a good job drawing. I like the detail you added to the people's faces.
- You really studied for your social studies test. You read the material over several times, outlined it and tested yourself on it. It really worked!
- I like the way you tried a lot of different strategies on that math problem until you finally got it.
- That was a hard English assignment, but you stuck with it until you got it done. You stayed at your desk and kept your concentration. That's great!
- I like that you took on that challenging project for your science class. It will take a lot of work—doing the research, designing the apparatus, making the parts and building it. You are going to learn a lot of great things.

Parents and teachers can also teach children to enjoy the process of learning by expressing positive views of challenges, effort and mistakes. Here are examples of such communications:

- Boy, this is hard—this is fun.
- Oh, sorry, that was too easy—no fun. Let's do something more challenging that you can learn from.
- Let's all talk about what we struggled with today and learned from. I'll go first.
- Mistakes are so interesting. Here's a wonderful mistake. Let's see what we can learn from it.   —C.S.D.

---

mind-set, we predicted, were destined for greater academic success and were quite likely to outperform their counterparts.

We validated these expectations in a study published in early 2007. Psychologists Lisa Blackwell of Columbia University and Kali H. Trzesniewski of Stanford University and I monitored 373 students for two years during the transition to junior high school, when the work gets more difficult and the grading more stringent, to determine how their mind-sets might affect their math grades. At the beginning of seventh grade, we assessed the students' mind-sets by asking them to agree or disagree with statements such as "Your intelligence is something very basic about you that you can't really change." We then assessed their beliefs about other aspects of learning and looked to see what happened to their grades.

As we had predicted, the students with a growth mind-set felt that learning was a more important goal in school than getting good grades. In addition, they held hard work in high regard, believing that the more you labored at something, the better you would become at it. They understood that even geniuses have to work hard for their great accomplishments. Confronted by a setback such as a disappointing test grade, students with a growth mind-set said they would study harder or try a different strategy for mastering the material.

The students who held a fixed mind-set, however, were concerned about looking smart with little regard for learning. They had negative views of effort, believing that having to work hard at something was a sign of low ability. They thought that a person with talent or intelligence did not need to work hard to do well. Attributing a bad grade to their own lack of ability, those with a fixed mind-set said that they would study *less* in the future, try never to take that subject again and consider cheating on future tests.

Such divergent outlooks had a dramatic impact on performance. At the start of junior high, the math achievement test scores of the students with a growth mind-set were comparable to those of students who displayed a fixed mind-set. But as the work became more difficult, the students with a growth mind-set showed greater persistence. As a result, their math grades overtook those of the other students by the end of the first semester—and the gap between the two groups continued to widen during the two years we followed them [see box on page 71].

Along with Columbia psychologist Heidi Grant, I found a similar relation between mind-set and achievement in a 2003 study of 128 Columbia freshman premed students who were enrolled in a challenging general chemistry course. Although all the students cared about grades, the ones who earned the best grades were those who placed a high premium on learning rather than on showing that they were smart in chemistry. The focus on learning strategies, effort and persistence paid off for these students.

Confronting Deficiencies

A belief in fixed intelligence also makes people less willing to admit to errors or to confront and remedy their deficiencies in school, at work and in their social relationships. In a study published in 1999 of 168 freshmen entering the University of Hong Kong, where all instruction and coursework are in English, three Hong Kong colleagues and I found that students with a growth mind-set who scored poorly on their English proficiency exam were far more inclined to take a remedial English course than were low-scoring students with a fixed mind-set. The students with a stagnant view of intelligence were presumably unwilling to admit to their deficit and thus passed up the opportunity to correct it.

A fixed mind-set can similarly hamper communication and progress in the workplace by leading managers and employees to discourage or ignore constructive criticism and advice. Research by psychologists Peter Heslin and Don VandeWalle of Southern Methodist University and Gary Latham of the University of Toronto shows that managers who have a fixed mind-set are less likely to seek or welcome feedback from their employees than are managers with a growth mind-set. Presumably, managers with a growth mind-set see themselves as works-in-progress and understand that they need feedback to improve, whereas bosses with a fixed mind-set are more likely to see criticism as reflecting their underlying

level of competence. Assuming that other people are not capable of changing either, executives with a fixed mind-set are also less likely to mentor their underlings. But after Heslin, VandeWalle and Latham gave managers a tutorial on the value and principles of the growth mind-set, supervisors became more willing to coach their employees and gave more useful advice.

Mind-set can affect the quality and longevity of personal relationships as well, through people's willingness—or unwillingness—to deal with difficulties. Those with a fixed mind-set are

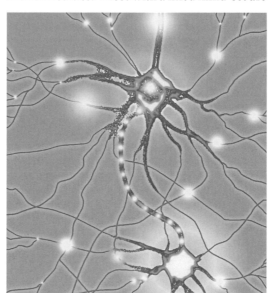

In tutorials that advance a growth mind-set, students discover that learning promotes the formation of new connections between neurons in the brain.

less likely than those with a growth mind-set to broach problems in their relationships and to try to solve them, according to a 2006 study I conducted with psychologist Lara Kammrath of Wilfrid Laurier University in Ontario. After all, if you think that human personality traits are more or less fixed, relationship repair seems largely futile. Individuals who believe people can change and grow, however, are more confident that confronting concerns in their relationships will lead to resolutions.

Proper Praise

How do we transmit a growth mind-set to our children? One way is by telling stories about achievements that result from hard work. For in-

(The Author)

CAROL S. DWECK is Lewis and Virginia Eaton Professor of Psychology at Stanford University. She has held professorships at Columbia University, the University of Illinois and Harvard University and is a member of the American Academy of Arts and Sciences. Her most recent book is *Mindset*, published by Random House in 2006.

stance, talking about math geniuses who were more or less born that way puts students in a fixed mind-set, but descriptions of great mathematicians who fell in love with math and developed amazing skills engenders a growth mind-set, our studies have shown. People also communicate mind-sets through praise [see box on page 72]. Although many, if not most, parents believe that they should build up a child by telling him or her how brilliant and talented he or she is, our research suggests that this is misguided.

In studies involving several hundred fifth graders published in 1998, for example, Columbia psychologist Claudia M. Mueller and I gave children questions from a nonverbal IQ test. After the first 10 problems, on which most children did fairly well, we praised them. We praised some of them for their intelligence: "Wow ... that's a really good score. You must be smart at this." We commended others for their effort: "Wow ... that's a really good score. You must have worked really hard."

We found that intelligence praise encouraged a fixed mind-set more often than did pats on the back for effort. Those congratulated for their intelligence, for example, shied away from a challenging assignment—they wanted an easy one instead—far more often than the kids applauded for their effort. (Most of those lauded for their hard work wanted the difficult problem set from which they would learn.) When we gave everyone hard problems anyway, those praised for being smart became discouraged, doubting their ability. And their scores, even on an easier problem set we gave them afterward, declined as compared with their previous results on equivalent problems. In contrast, students praised for their effort did not lose confidence when faced with the harder questions, and their performance improved markedly on the easier problems that followed [see box on opposite page].

Making Up Your Mind-set

In addition to encouraging a growth mind-set through praise for effort, parents and teachers can help children by providing explicit instruction regarding the mind as a learning machine. Blackwell, Trzesniewski and I recently designed an eight-session workshop for 91 students whose math grades were declining in their first year of junior high. Forty-eight of the students received instruction in study skills only, whereas the others attended a combination of study skills sessions and classes in which they learned about the growth mind-set and how to apply it to schoolwork.

In the growth mind-set classes, students read and discussed an article entitled "You Can Grow Your Brain." They were taught that the brain is like a muscle that gets stronger with use and that learning prompts neurons in the brain to grow new connections. From such instruction, many students began to see themselves as agents of their own brain development. Students who had been disruptive or bored sat still and took note. One particularly unruly boy looked up during the discussion and said, "You mean I don't have to be dumb?"

As the semester progressed, the math grades of the kids who learned only study skills continued to

Chemist Marie Curie (*left*) and inventor Thomas A. Edison (*right*) developed their genius through passion and tremendous effort.

decline, whereas those of the students given the growth-mind-set training stopped falling and began to bounce back to their former levels. Despite being unaware that there were two types of instruction, teachers reported noticing significant motivational changes in 27 percent of the children in the growth mind-set workshop as compared with only 9 percent of students in the control group. One teacher wrote: "Your workshop has already had an effect. L [our unruly male student], who never puts in any extra effort and often doesn't turn in homework on time, actually stayed up late to finish an assignment early so I could review it and give him a chance to revise it. He earned a B+. (He had been getting Cs and lower.)"

Other researchers have replicated our results. Psychologists Catherine Good, then at Columbia, and Joshua Aronson and Michael Inzlicht of New York University reported in 2003 that a growth mind-set workshop raised the math and English achievement test scores of seventh graders. In a 2002 study Aronson, Good (then a graduate student at the University of Texas at Austin) and their colleagues found that college students began to enjoy their schoolwork more, value it more highly and get better grades as a result of training that fostered a growth mind-set.

We have now encapsulated such instruction in an interactive computer program called "Brainology," which should be more widely available by mid-2008. Its six modules teach students about the brain—what it does and how to make it work better. In a virtual brain lab, users can click on brain regions to determine their functions or on nerve endings to see how connections form when people learn. Users can also advise virtual students with problems as a way of practicing how to handle schoolwork difficulties; additionally, users keep an online journal of their study practices.

New York City seventh graders who tested a pilot version of Brainology told us that the program had changed their view of learning and how to promote it. One wrote: "My favorite thing from Brainology is the neurons part where when u [sic] learn something there are connections and they keep growing. I always picture them when I'm in school." A teacher said of the students who used the program: "They offer to practice, study, take notes, or pay attention to ensure that connections will be made."

Teaching children such information is not just a ploy to get them to study. People do differ in intelligence, talent and ability. And yet research is converging on the conclusion that great accom-

The Effects of Praise

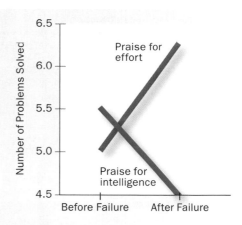

Children praised for their intelligence solved significantly fewer problems after a failure than they had before encountering difficulty. In contrast, children praised for their effort solved *more* problems after their brush with adversity than they had before it.

plishment, and even what we call genius, is typically the result of years of passion and dedication and not something that flows naturally from a gift. Mozart, Edison, Curie, Darwin and Cézanne were not simply born with talent; they cultivated it through tremendous and sustained effort. Similarly, hard work and discipline contribute much more to school achievement than IQ does.

Such lessons apply to almost every human endeavor. For instance, many young athletes value talent more than hard work and have consequently become unteachable. Similarly, many people accomplish little in their jobs without constant praise and encouragement to maintain their motivation. If we foster a growth mind-set in our homes and schools, however, we will give our children the tools to succeed in their pursuits and to become responsible employees and citizens. **M**

(Further Reading)

◆ **Praise for Intelligence Can Undermine Children's Motivation and Performance.** Claudia M. Mueller and Carol S. Dweck in *Journal of Personality and Social Psychology,* Vol. 75, No. 1, pages 33–52; November 1998.

◆ **Self-Discipline Outdoes IQ in Predicting Academic Performance of Adolescents.** A. Duckworth and M. Seligman in *Psychological Science,* Vol. 16, pages 939–944; 2005.

◆ **Why Do Beliefs about Intelligence Influence Learning Success? A Social Cognitive Neuroscience Model.** J. A. Mangels, B. Butterfield, J. Lamb, C. Good and C. S. Dweck in *Social Cognitive and Affective Neuroscience,* Vol. 1, No. 2, pages 75–86; September 2006.

◆ **The Cambridge Handbook of Expertise and Expert Performance.** Edited by K. A. Ericsson, N. Charness, P. J. Feltovich and R. R. Hoffman. Cambridge University Press, 2006.

◆ **Implicit Theories of Intelligence Predict Achievement across an Adolescent Transition: A Longitudinal Study and an Intervention.** Lisa S. Blackwell, Kali H. Trzesniewski and Carol S. Dweck in *Child Development,* Vol. 78, No. 1, pages 246–263; January/February 2007.

◆ **Subtle Linguistic Cues Affect Children's Motivation.** A. Cimpian, H.-M. C. Arce, E. M. Markman and C. S. Dweck in *Psychological Science,* Vol. 18, No. 4, pages 314–316; April 2007.

AND C. S. DWECK, IN JOURNAL OF PERSONALITY AND SOCIAL PSYCHOLOGY, VOL. 75, NO. 1; JULY 1998

Bisexual Species

Homosexual behavior is surprisingly common in the animal kingdom. It may be adaptive—helping animals to get along, maintain fecundity and protect their young

By Emily V. Driscoll

Two penguins native to Antarctica met one spring day in 1998 in a tank at the Central Park Zoo in midtown Manhattan. They perched atop stones and took turns diving in and out of the clear water below. They entwined necks, called to each other and mated. They then built a nest together to prepare for an egg. But no egg was forthcoming: Roy and Silo were both male.

Robert Gramzay, a keeper at the zoo, watched the chinstrap penguin pair roll a rock into their nest and sit on it, according to newspaper reports. Gramzay found an egg from another pair of penguins that was having difficulty hatching it and slipped it into Roy and Silo's nest. Roy and Silo took turns warming the egg with their blubbery underbellies until, after 34 days, a female chick pecked her way into the world. Roy and Silo kept the gray, fuzzy chick warm and regurgitated food into her tiny black beak.

Like most animal species, penguins tend to pair with the opposite sex, for the obvious reason. But researchers are finding that same-sex couplings are surprisingly widespread in the animal kingdom. Roy and Silo belong to one of as many as 1,500 species of wild and captive animals that have been observed engaging in homosexual activity. Researchers have seen such same-sex goings-on in both male and female, old and young, and social and solitary creatures and on branches of the evolutionary tree ranging from insects to mammals.

Recent same-sex couplings at New York's Central Park Zoo include these two young male chinstrap penguins, Squawk and Milo.

Unlike most humans, however, individual animals generally cannot be classified as gay or straight: an animal that engages in a same-sex flirtation or partnership does not necessarily shun heterosexual encounters. Rather many species seem to have ingrained homosexual tendencies that are a regular part of their society. That is, there are probably no strictly gay critters, just bisexual ones. "Animals don't do sexual identity. They just do sex," says sociologist Eric Anderson of the University of Bath in England.

Nevertheless, the study of homosexual activity in diverse species may elucidate the evolutionary origins of such behavior. Researchers are now revealing, for example, that animals may engage in same-sex couplings to diffuse social tensions, to better protect their young or to maintain fecundity when opposite-sex partners are unavailable—or simply because it is fun. These observations suggest to some that bisexuality is a natural state among animals, perhaps *Homo sapiens* included, despite the sexual-orientation boundaries most people take for granted. "[In humans] the categories of gay and straight are socially constructed," Anderson says.

What is more, homosexuality among some species, including penguins, appears to be far more common in captivity than in the wild. Captivity, scientists say, may bring out gay behaviors in part because of a scarcity of opposite-sex mates. In addition, an enclosed environment boosts an animal's stress levels, leading to a

"The more homosexuality, **the more peaceful** the species," one specialist says. "Bonobos are peaceful."

Female homosexual encounters among bonobos help the apes get along: they resolve conflicts and promote bonding.

greater urge to relieve the stress. Some of the same influences may encourage what some researchers call "situational homosexuality" in humans in same-sex settings such as prisons or sports teams.

Making Peace

Modern studies of animal homosexuality date to the late 19th century with observations on in-

FAST FACTS
Fit to Be Gay

1 » Same-sex couplings are surprisingly widespread in the animal kingdom. Observers have witnessed as many as 1,500 species of wild and captive animals engaging in homosexual activity.

2 » Animals may engage in homosexual acts to diffuse social tensions, to better protect their young or to maintain fecundity when opposite-sex partners are unavailable—or simply because it is fun.

3 » Homosexuality among some species appears to be far more common in captivity than in the wild. Captivity may bring out gay behaviors because of a lack of opposite-sex mates and a greater need for stress relief.

sects and small animals. In 1896, for example, French entomologist Henri Gadeau de Kerville of the Society of Friends of Natural Sciences and the Museum of Rouen published a drawing of two male scarab beetles copulating. Then, during the first half of the 1900s, various investigators described homosexual behavior in baboons, garter snakes and gentoo penguins, among other species. Back then, scientists generally considered homosexual acts among animals to be abnormal. In some cases, they "treated" the animals by, say, castrating them or giving them lobotomies.

At least one early report, however, was more than descriptive, yielding insight into the possible origins of the behavior. In a 1914 lab experiment Gilbert Van Tassel Hamilton, a psychopathologist practicing in Montecito, Calif., reported that same-sex behavior in 20 Japanese macaques and two baboons occurred largely as a way of making peace with would-be foes. In the *Journal of Animal Behavior* Hamilton observed that females offered sex to the more dominant macaques of the same sex: "homosexual behavior is of relatively frequent occurrence in the female when she is threatened by another female, but it is rarely manifested in response to sexual hunger." And in males, he penned, "homosexual alliances between mature and immature males may possess a defensive value for immature males, since they insure the assistance of an adult defender in the event of an attack."

More recently, some researchers studying bonobos (close relatives of the chimpanzee) have come to similar conclusions. Bonobos are highly promiscuous, and about half their sexual activity involves same-sex partners. Female bonobos rub one another's genitals so often that some scientists have suggested that their genitalia evolved to facilitate this activity. The female bonobo's clitoris is "frontally placed, perhaps because selection favored a position maximizing stimulation during the genital-genital rubbing common among females," wrote behavioral ecologist Marlene Zuk of the University of California, Riverside, in her 2002 book *Sexual Selections: What We Can and Can't Learn about Sex from Animals*. Male bonobos have been observed to mount, fondle and even perform oral sex on one another.

Such behavior seems to ease social tensions. In *Bonobo: The Forgotten Ape* (University of California Press, 1997), Emory University primatologist Frans B. M. de Waal and his co-author photographer Frans Lanting wrote that "when one female has hit a juvenile and the juvenile's mother has come to its defense, the problem may be resolved by intense GG-rubbing between the two adults." De Waal has observed hundreds of such incidents, suggesting that these homosexual acts may be a general peacekeeping strategy. "The more homosexuality, the more peaceful the species," asserts Petter Böckman, an academic adviser at the University of Oslo's Museum of Natural History in Norway. "Bonobos are peaceful."

In fact, such acts are so essential to bonobo socialization that they constitute a rite of passage for young females into adulthood. Bonobos live together in groups of about 60 in a matriarchal system. Females leave the group during adolescence and gain admission to another bonobo clan through grooming and sexual encounters with other females. These behaviors promote bonding and give the new recruits benefits such as protection and access to food.

Defended Nest

In some birds, same-sex unions, particularly between males, might have evolved as a parenting strategy to increase the survival of their young. "In black swans, if two males find each other and make a nest, they'll be very successful at nest making because they are bigger and stronger than a male and female," Böckman says. In such cases, he says, "having a same-sex partner will actually pay off as a sensible life strategy."

In other instances, homosexual bonding between female parents can boost the survival of offspring when male-female pairings are not possible. In birds called oystercatchers, intense competition for male mates would leave some females single were it not for polygamous trios. In a study published in 1998 in *Nature,* zoologist Dik Heg and geneticist Rob van Treuren, both then at the University of Groningen in the Netherlands, observed that roughly 2 percent of oystercatcher breeding groups consist of two females and a male. In some of these families, Heg and van Treuren found, the females tend separate nests and fight over the male, but in others, all three birds watch over a single nest. In the latter case, the females bond by mounting each other as well as the male. The cooperative triangles produce more offspring than the competitive ones, because such nests are better tended and protected from predators.

Such arrangements point to the evolutionary fitness of stable social relationships, whatever their type. Biologist Joan E. Roughgarden of Stanford University believes that evolutionary biologists tend to adhere too strongly to Darwin's theory of sexual selection and have thus largely overlooked the importance of bonding and friendship to animal societies and the survival of their young. "[Darwin] equated reproduction with finding a mate rather than paying attention to how the offspring are naturally reared," Roughgarden says.

Protection of progeny, social bonding and conflict avoidance may not be the only reasons animals naturally come to same-sex relationships. Many animals do it simply "because they want to," Böckman says. "People view animals as robots who behave as their genes say, but animals have feelings, and they react to those feelings." He adds that "as long as they feel the urge [for sex], they'll go for it."

A recent finding indicates that homosexual behavior may be so common because it is rooted in an animal's brain wiring—at least in the case of fruit flies. In a study appearing earlier this year in *Nature Neuroscience,* neuroscientist David E. Featherstone of the University of Illinois at Chicago and his colleagues found that they could switch on homosexual leanings in fruit flies by manipulating a gene for a protein they call "genderblind," which regulates communication between neurons that secrete and respond to the neurotransmitter glutamate.

Males that carried the mutant *genderblind* gene—which depressed levels of the protein by about two thirds—were uncharacteristically attracted to the chemical cues exuded by other males. As a result, these mutant males courted and attempted to copulate with other males. The finding suggests that wild fruit flies may be prewired for both heterosexual and homosexual behavior, the authors write, but that the genderblind protein suppresses the glutamate-

Up to one quarter of black swan families include parents of the same sex.

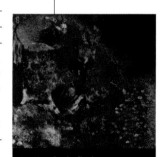

In the fruit fly brain (*shown in cross section*), the protein genderblind (*purple*) abuts neurons that communicate using the neurotransmitter glutamate (*green*), a pattern consistent with the idea that genderblind influences a fly's sexual preference by modulating glutamate signaling.

(The Author)

EMILY V. DRISCOLL is a freelance science writer living in New York City.

ACCESS TO WORKING MEMORY, BY FIONA MCNAB AND TORKE L. KLINGBERG, IN NATURE NEUROSCIENCE, VOL. 11, NO. 1; JANUARY 2008 (bottom)

based circuits that promote homosexual behavior. Such brain architecture may enable same-sex behavior to surface easily, supporting the notion that it might confer an evolutionary advantage in some circumstances.

The Captivity Effect

In some less social species, homosexual behavior is almost unheard of in wild animals but may surface in captivity. Wild koalas, which are mostly solitary, seem to be strictly heterosexual. But in a 2007 study veterinary scientist Clive J. C. Phillips of the University of Queensland in Brisbane, Australia, and his colleagues observed 43 instances of homosexual activity among female koalas living in a same-sex enclosure at the Lone Pine Koala Sanctuary. The captive females shrieked male mating calls and mated with one another, sometimes participating in multiple encounters of up to five koalas. "The behavior in captivity was certainly enhanced in terms of homosexual activity," Phillips says.

He believes that the females acted this way in part because of stress. Animals often experience stress in enclosed habitats and may engage in homosexual behavior to relieve that tension. A lack of male partners probably also played a role, Phillips suggests. When female koalas are in heat, their ovaries release the sex hormone estrogen, which triggers mating behavior—whether or not

Wild koalas are heterosexual, but females living together in captivity in Brisbane, Australia, shrieked male mating calls and mated with one another.

males are present. This hardwired urge to copulate, even if expressed with a female partner, might be adaptive. "The homosexual behavior preserves sexual function," Phillips says, enabling an animal to maintain its reproductive fitness and interest in sexual activity. In males, this benefit is even more obvious: homosexual behavior stimulates the continued production of seminal fluid.

A lack of opposite-sex partners is also thought to help explain the prevalence of homosexuality among penguins in zoos. In addition to several gay penguin couplings in the U.S., 20 same-sex penguin partnerships were formed in 2004 in zoos in Japan. Such behavior "is very rare in penguins' natural habitats," says animal ecologist Keisuke Ueda of Rikkyo University in Tokyo. Thus, Ueda speculates that the behavior—which included both male pairings and female couplings—arose as a result of the skewed sex ratios at zoos.

Researchers have found still other reasons for homosexual behavior in domesticated cattle—which is such a common occurrence that farmers and animal breeders have developed terms for it. "Bulling" refers to male pairs mounting, and "going boaring" is its female counterpart. For cows, the behavior is not just a stress reliever. It is a way to signal sexual receptivity. The females mount

Let Them Be Gay

Sometimes zookeepers do not know how to react to their animals' homosexual behavior. In 2005 workers at Bremerhaven's Zoo on the Sea in Germany discovered that three of their five endangered Humboldt penguin couples were of the same sex. The keepers brought in four female Humboldt penguins from Sweden in hopes of tempting the males. That action angered gay and lesbian groups around the world. In a letter to Bremerhaven's mayor Jörg Schulz, a group of European gay activists protested what they called "organized and forced harassment through female seductresses."

In the end, the males were not swayed anyway. "The males have scarcely thrown the females a single glance," said zoo director Heike Kück to the German magazine *Der Spiegel*. So more males were flown in to keep the Swedish females company.
—E.V.D.

one another to signal their readiness to mate to the bulls—which, in captivity, may cause a breeder to know when to bring in a suitable opposite-sex partner.

Homosexual mounting is much rarer among cattle in the wild, Phillips asserts, based on his research on gaurs in Malaysia, a wild counterpart to domesticated cattle. "Cattle evolved in the forest, so a visual signal was not going to be useful for them," he says.

Stress and the greater availability of same-sex partners may similarly contribute to the practice of homosexual acts among self-described heterosexual humans in environments such as the military, jails and sports teams. In a study published this year in the journal *Sex Roles*, Anderson found that 40 percent of 49 heterosexual former high school football players attending various U.S. universities had had at least one homosexual encounter. These ranged from kissing to oral sex to threesomes that included a woman. In team sports, homosexuality is "no big deal and it increases cohesion among members of that team," Anderson claims. "It feels good, and [the athletes] bond."

In stressful same-sex environments such as prisons or a war zone, heterosexuals may engage in homosexual behavior in part to relieve tension. "Homosexuality appears mostly in social species," Böckman says. "It makes flock life easier, and jail flock life is very difficult."

Altered Spaces

In recent decades zoo officials have tried to minimize the stresses of captivity by making their enclosures more like animals' natural habitats. In the 1950s zoo animals lived behind bars in barren enclosures. But since the late 1970s zoo homes have become more hospitable, including more open space, along with plants and murals representative of an animal's natural habitat. The Association of Zoos and Aquariums (AZA) regulates everything from cage dimensions to animal bedding. The AZA also outlines enrichment activities for captive creatures: for instance, two golden brown Amur leopards at the Staten Island Zoo regularly play with a papier-mâché zebra, an animal they have never seen in the flesh.

Researchers hope such improvements might affect animal behavior, making it more like what occurs in the wild. One possible sign of more hospitable conditions might be a rate of homosexuality more in line with that of wild members of the same species. Some people, however, contest the notion that zookeepers should prevent or discourage homosexual behavior among the an-

In 2004 Silo (*right*) deserted his longtime male partner, Roy (*not shown*), for a female chinstrap penguin named Scrappy (*left*).

imals they care for [*see box on opposite page*].

And whereas captivity may engender what appears to be an unnaturally high level of homosexual activity in some animal species, human same-sex environments might bring out normal tendencies that other settings tend to suppress. That is, some experts argue that humans, like some other animals, are naturally bisexual. "We should be calling humans bisexual because this idea of exclusive homosexuality is not accurate of people," Roughgarden says. "Homosexuality is mixed in with heterosexuality across cultures and history."

Even Silo the penguin, who had been coupled with Roy for six years, displayed this malleability of sexual orientation. One spring day in 2004 a female chinstrap penguin named Scrappy—a transplant from SeaWorld in San Diego—caught his eye, and he abruptly left Roy for her. Meanwhile Roy and Silo's "daughter," Tango, carried on in the tradition of her fathers. Her chosen mate: a female named Tazuni. **M**

(Further Reading)

◆ **Bonobo: The Forgotten Ape.** Frans B. M. de Waal and Frans Lanting. University of California Press, 1997.
◆ **Biological Exuberance.** Bruce Bagemihl. St. Martin's Press, 1999.
◆ **Evolution's Rainbow: Diversity, Gender, and Sexuality in Nature and People.** Joan Roughgarden. University of California Press, 2004.
◆ **Heterosexual and Homosexual Behaviour and Vocalisations in Captive Female Koalas (*Phascolarctos cinereus*).** Stacey Feige, Kate Nilsson, Clive J. C. Phillips and Steve D. Johnston in *Applied Animal Behaviour Science*, Vol. 103, Nos. 1–2, pages 131–145; 2007.

The brain and the immune system
continuously signal each other, often along
the same pathways, which may explain
how state of mind influences health

The Mind-Body
Interaction
in Disease

By Esther M. Sternberg and Philip W. Gold

The belief that the mind plays an important role in physical illness goes back to the

earliest days of medicine. From the time of the ancient Greeks to the beginning of the 20th century, it was generally accepted by both physician and patient that the mind can affect the course of illness, and it seemed natural to apply this concept in medical treatments of disease. After the discovery of antibiotics, a new assumption arose that treatment of infectious or inflammatory disease requires only the elimination of the foreign organism or agent that triggers the illness. In the rush to discover antibiotics and drugs that cure specific infections and diseases, the fact that the body's own responses can influence susceptibility to disease and its course was largely ignored by medical researchers.

It is ironic that research into infectious and inflammatory disease first led 20th-century medicine to reject the idea that the mind influences physical illness, and now research in the same field—including the work of our laboratories and of our collaborators at the National Institutes of Health—is proving the contrary. New molecular and pharmacological tools have made it possible for us to identify the intricate network that exists between the immune system and the brain, a network that allows the two systems to signal each other continuously and rapidly. Chemicals produced by immune cells signal the brain, and the brain in turn sends chemical signals to restrain the immune system. These same chemical signals also affect behavior and the response to stress. Disruption of this communication network in any way, whether inherited or through drugs,

IMMUNE RESPONSE can be altered at the cellular level by stress hormones.

toxic substances or surgery, exacerbates the diseases that these systems guard against: infectious, inflammatory, autoimmune, and associated mood disorders.

The clinical significance of these findings is likely to prove profound. They hold the promise of extending the range of therapeutic treatments available for various disorders, as drugs previously known to work primarily for nervous system problems are shown to be effective against immune maladies, and vice versa. They also help to substantiate the popularly held impression (still discounted in some medical circles) that our state of mind can influence how well we resist or recover from infectious or inflammatory diseases.

The brain's stress response system is activated in threatening situations. The immune system responds automatically to pathogens and foreign molecules. These two response systems are the body's principal means for maintaining an internal steady state called homeostasis. A substantial proportion of human cellular machinery is dedicated to maintaining it.

When homeostasis is disturbed or threatened, a repertoire of molecular, cellular and behavioral responses comes into play. These responses attempt to counteract the disturbing forces in order to reestablish a steady state. They can be specific to the foreign invader or a particular stress, or they can be generalized and nonspecific when the threat to homeostasis exceeds a certain threshold. The adaptive responses may themselves

Updated from The Mysteries of the Mind *(Special Issue, 1997)*

ANATOMY OF THE STRESS AND IMMUNE SYSTEMS

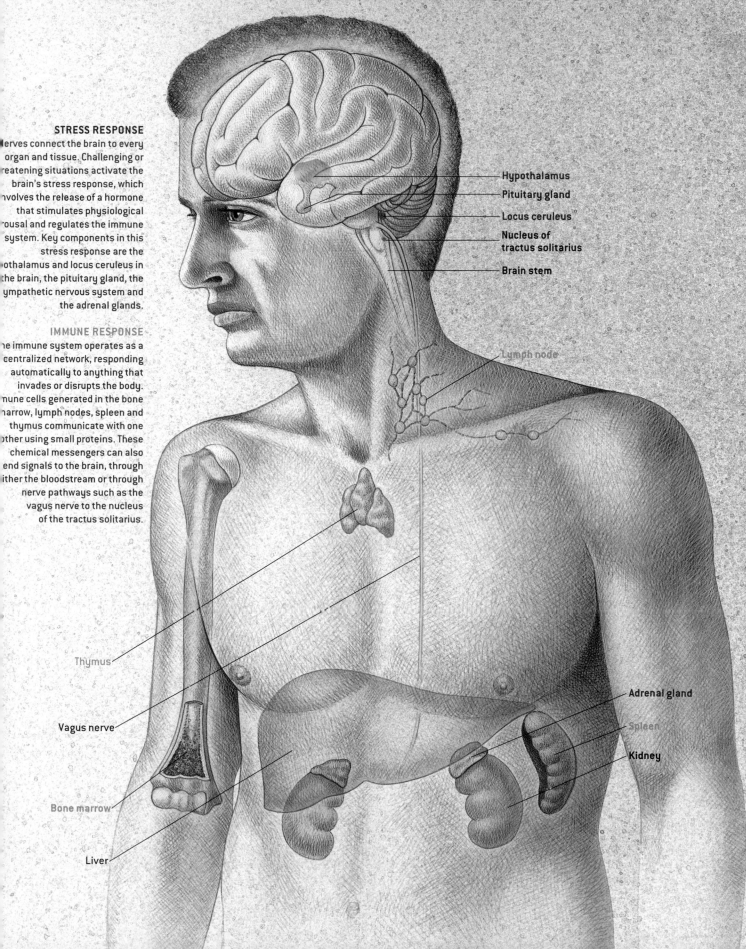

STRESS RESPONSE

Nerves connect the brain to every organ and tissue. Challenging or threatening situations activate the brain's stress response, which involves the release of a hormone that stimulates physiological arousal and regulates the immune system. Key components in this stress response are the hypothalamus and locus ceruleus in the brain, the pituitary gland, the sympathetic nervous system and the adrenal glands.

IMMUNE RESPONSE

The immune system operates as a decentralized network, responding automatically to anything that invades or disrupts the body. Immune cells generated in the bone marrow, lymph nodes, spleen and thymus communicate with one other using small proteins. These chemical messengers can also send signals to the brain, through either the bloodstream or through nerve pathways such as the vagus nerve to the nucleus of the tractus solitarius.

Hypothalamus

Pituitary gland

Locus ceruleus

Nucleus of tractus solitarius

Brain stem

Lymph node

Thymus

Vagus nerve

Bone marrow

Liver

Adrenal gland

Spleen

Kidney

turn into stressors capable of producing disease. We are just beginning to understand the interdependence of the brain and the immune system, how they help to regulate and counterregulate each other and how they themselves can malfunction and produce disease.

The stress response promotes physiological and behavioral changes in threatening or taxing situations. For instance, when we are facing a potentially life-threatening situation, the brain's stress response goes into action to enhance our focused attention, our fear and our fight-or-flight response, while inhibiting behaviors, such as feeding, sex and sleep, that might lessen the chance of immediate survival. The stress response, however, must be

The central nervous and immune systems, however, are more similar than different in their modes of receiving, recognizing and integrating various signals and in their structural design for accomplishing these tasks. Both the central nervous system and the immune system possess "sensory" elements, which receive information from the environment and other parts of the body, and "motor" elements, which carry out an appropriate response.

Cross Communication

BOTH SYSTEMS also rely on chemical mediators for communication. Electrical signals along nerve pathways, for instance, are converted to chemical signals at the synapses between neurons. The

to the pituitary gland, which lies just beneath the brain. CRH causes the pituitary to release adrenocorticotropin hormone (ACTH) into the bloodstream, which stimulates the adrenal glands to produce cortisol, the best-known stress hormone.

Cortisol is a steroid hormone that increases the rate and strength of heart contractions, sensitizes blood vessels to the actions of norepinephrine (an adrenaline-like hormone) and affects many metabolic functions—actions that help the body meet a stressful situation. In addition, cortisol is a potent immunoregulator and anti-inflammatory agent. It plays a crucial role in preventing the immune system from overreacting to injuries and damaging tissues. Furthermore, cortisol inhibits

The ADAPTIVE RESPONSES may themselves turn into stressors capable of PRODUCING DISEASE.

regulated to be neither excessive nor suboptimal; otherwise, disorders of arousal, thought and feeling emerge.

The immune system's job is to bar foreign pathogens from the body and to recognize and destroy those that penetrate its shield. The immune system must also neutralize potentially dangerous toxins, facilitate repair of damaged or worn tissues, and dispose of abnormal cells. Its responses are so powerful that they require constant regulation to ensure that they are neither excessive nor indiscriminate and yet remain effective. When the immune system escapes regulation, autoimmune and inflammatory diseases or immune deficiency syndromes result.

The immune and central nervous systems appear, at first glance, to be organized in very different ways. The brain is usually regarded as a centralized command center, sending and receiving electrical signals along fixed pathways, much like a telephone network. In contrast, the immune system is decentralized, and its organs (spleen, lymph nodes, thymus and bone marrow) are located throughout the body. The classical view is that the immune system communicates by releasing immune cells into the bloodstream that travel to new locations to deliver their messages or to perform other functions.

chemical messengers produced by immune cells communicate not only with other parts of the immune system but also with the brain and nerves. Chemicals released by nerve cells can act as signals to immune cells. Hormones from the body travel to the brain in the bloodstream, and the brain itself makes hormones. Indeed, the brain is perhaps the most prolific endocrine organ in the body and produces many hormones that act both on the brain and on tissues throughout the body.

A key hormone shared by the central nervous and immune systems is corticotropin-releasing hormone (CRH); produced in the hypothalamus and several other brain regions, it unites the stress and immune responses. The hypothalamus releases CRH into a specialized bloodstream circuit that conveys the hormone

the release of CRH by the hypothalamus—which keeps this component of the stress response under control. Thus, CRH and cortisol directly link the body's brain-regulated stress response and its immune response.

CRH-secreting neurons of the hypothalamus send fibers to regions in the brain stem that help to regulate the sympathetic nervous system, as well as to another brain stem area called the locus ceruleus. The sympathetic nervous system, which mobilizes the body during stress, also innervates immune organs, such as the thymus, lymph nodes and spleen, and helps to control inflammatory responses throughout the body. Stimulation of the locus ceruleus leads to behavioral arousal, fear and enhanced vigilance. Perhaps even more important for the

THE AUTHORS

ESTHER M. STERNBERG and PHILIP W. GOLD carry out their research on stress and immune systems at the National Institute of Mental Health. Sternberg is chief of the section on neuroendocrine immunology and behavior and director of the Integrative Neural Immune Program, and Gold is chief of the clinical neuroendocrinology branch. Sternberg received her M.D. from McGill University. Her work on the mechanisms and molecular basis of neural immune communication has led to a growing recognition of the importance of mind-body interaction. She is also the author of The Balance Within: The Science Connecting Health and Emotions (2000). Before joining the NIMH in 1974, Gold received his medical training at Duke University and Harvard University. He and his group were among the first to introduce data implicating corticotropin-releasing hormone and its related hormones in the pathophysiology of melancholic and atypical depression and in the mechanisms of action of antidepressant drugs.

induction of fear-related behaviors is the amygdala, where inputs from the sensory regions of the brain are charged as stressful or not. CRH-secreting neurons in the central nucleus of the amygdala send fibers to the hypothalamus, the locus ceruleus, and to other parts of the brain stem. These CRH-secreting neurons are targets of messengers released by immune cells during an immune response. By recruiting the CRH-secreting neurons, the immune signals not only activate cortisol-mediated restraint of the immune response but also induce behaviors that assist in recovery from illness or injury. CRH-secreting neurons also have connections with hypothalamic regions that regulate food intake and reproductive behavior. In addition, other hormonal and nerve systems—such as the thyroid, growth and female sex hormones, and the sympathomedullary pathways (connections of the sympathetic nervous system and medulla)—influence interactions between the brain and the immune system.

Immune System Signals

THE IMMUNE RESPONSE is an elegant and finely tuned cascade of cellular events aimed at ridding the body of foreign substances, bacteria and viruses. One of the major discoveries of contemporary immunology is that white blood cells produce small proteins that indirectly coordinate the responses of other parts of the immune system to pathogens.

For example, the protein interleukin-1 (IL-1) is made by a type of white blood cell called a monocyte or macrophage. IL-1 stimulates another type of white blood cell, the lymphocyte, to produce interleukin-2 (IL-2), which in turn induces lymphocytes to develop into mature immune cells. Some mature lymphocytes, called plasma cells, make antibodies that fight infection, whereas others, the cytotoxic lymphocytes, kill viruses directly. Other interleukins mediate the activation of immune cells that are involved in allergic reactions.

The interleukins were originally named for what was considered to be their primary function: communication among ("inter-") the white blood cells ("leukins"). But interleukins also act as chemical signals among immune cells and

many other types of cells and organs, including parts of the brain. Cytokines is the more general term for biological molecules that many different kinds of cells use to communicate. Each cytokine is a distinct protein molecule, encoded by a separate gene, that targets a particular cell type. A cytokine can either stimulate or inhibit a response depending on the presence of other cytokines or other stimuli and the current state of metabolic activity. This flexibility allows the immune system to take the most appropriate actions to stabilize the local cellular environment and to maintain homeostasis.

Cytokines from the body's immune system can send signals to the brain in several ways. Ordinarily, a "blood-brain barrier" shields the central nervous system from potentially dangerous molecules in the bloodstream. During inflammation or illness, however, this barrier

becomes more permeable, and cytokines may be carried across into the brain with nutrients from the blood. Certain cytokines, on the other hand, readily pass through leaky areas in the blood-brain barrier at any time. But cytokines do not have to cross the blood-brain barrier to exert their effects. Cytokines can attach to their receptors in the lining of blood vessels in the brain and stimulate the release of secondary chemical signals in the brain tissue around the blood vessels.

Cytokines can also signal the brain via direct nerve routes, such as the vagus nerve, which innervates the heart, stomach, small intestine and other organs of the abdominal cavity. Injection of IL-1 into the abdominal cavity activates the nucleus of the tractus solitarius, the principal region of the brain stem for receipt of visceral sensory signals. Cutting the vagus nerve blocks activation of this brain

STRESS RESPONSE SYSTEM

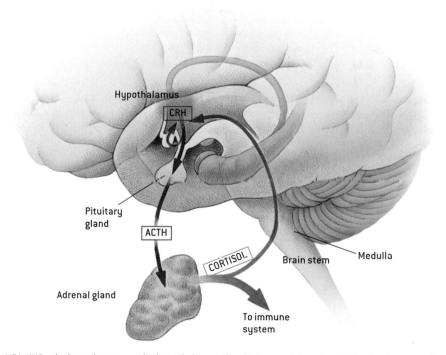

HPA AXIS—the interplay among the hypothalamus, the pituitary and the adrenal glands—is a central component of the brain's neuroendocrine response to stress. The hypothalamus, when stimulated, secretes corticotropin-releasing hormone (CRH) into the hypophyseal portal system, which supplies blood to the anterior pituitary. CRH stimulates the pituitary (red arrows show stimulatory pathways) to secrete adrenocorticotropin hormone (ACTH) into the bloodstream. ACTH causes the adrenal glands to release cortisol, the classic stress hormone that arouses the body to meet a challenging situation. But cortisol then modulates the stress response (blue arrows indicate inhibitory effects) by acting on the hypothalamus to inhibit the continued release of CRH. Also a potent immunoregulator, cortisol acts on many parts of the immune system to prevent it from overreacting and harming healthy cells and tissue.

nucleus by IL-1. Sending signals along nerve routes is the most rapid mechanism—on the order of milliseconds—by which cytokines signal the brain.

Activation of the brain by cytokines from the peripheral parts of the body induces behaviors of the stress response, such as anxiety and cautious avoidance, that keep an individual out of harm's way until full healing occurs. Anyone who has experienced lethargy and excess sleepiness during an illness will recognize this set of responses as "sickness behavior."

brain tissue of patients living with AIDS, concentrated in areas around the giant macrophages that invade the patients' brain tissue. Immune factors, however, are not always toxic to neurons. Specific activated T lymphocytes play an important role in preventing neuronal cell death after injury. This discovery is leading to new approaches to treating and preventing paralysis following spinal cord injury.

Any disruption of communication between the brain and the immune system leads to greater susceptibility to in-

ders them highly susceptible. Further proof comes from studies in which the transplantation of hypothalamic tissue from disease-resistant rats into the brain of susceptible rats improves their resistance to peripheral inflammation.

These animal studies demonstrate that disruption of the brain's stress response enhances the body's response to inflammatory disease, and reconstitution of the stress response reduces susceptibility to inflammation. One implication of these findings is that disruption of the

The IMMUNE RESPONSE is an elegant and finely tuned cascade of cellular events aimed at ridding the body of FOREIGN SUBSTANCES.

Indeed, patients receiving cytokine treatment for immunosuppression in cancer and AIDS may experience symptoms of depression and even suicidality. These symptoms can be prevented by pretreatment with antidepressants.

Neurons and nonneuronal brain cells also produce cytokines. Cytokines in the brain regulate nerve cell growth and death and can be recruited by the immune system to stimulate the release of CRH. Some have proposed that brain cytokines may play a role in symptoms of depression in the absence of known sickness or infection. The IL-1 cytokine system in the brain is currently the best understood—all its components have been identified, including receptors and a naturally occurring antagonist that binds to IL-1 receptors without activating them. The anatomical and cellular locations of such cytokine circuitry are being mapped out in detail, and this knowledge will aid researchers in designing drugs that block or enhance the actions of such circuits and the functions they regulate.

Excessive amounts of cytokines in the brain can be toxic to nerves. In genetically engineered mice, inserted genes that overexpress cytokines produce neurotoxic effects. Some of the neurological symptoms of AIDS in humans may also be caused by overexpression of certain cytokines in the brain. High levels of IL-1 and other cytokines have been found in the

flammatory disease and, frequently, to increased immune complications. For instance, animals whose brain-immune communications have been disrupted (through surgery or drugs) are highly liable to lethal complications of inflammatory diseases and infectious diseases.

Susceptibility to inflammatory disease that is associated with genetically impaired stress response can be found across species—in rats, mice, chickens and, though the evidence is less direct, humans. For instance, the Lewis strain of rat is naturally prone to many inflammatory diseases because of a severe impairment of its HPA (for hypothalamus, pituitary and adrenal) axis, which greatly diminishes CRH secretion in response to stress. In contrast, the hyperresponsive HPA axis in the Fischer strain of rat provides it with a strong resistance to inflammatory disease.

Evidence of a causal link between an impaired stress response and susceptibility to inflammatory disease comes from pharmacological and surgical studies. Pharmacological intervention such as treatment with a drug that blocks cortisol receptors enhances autoimmune inflammatory disease. Injecting low doses of cortisol into disease-susceptible rats enhances their resistance to inflammation. Strong evidence comes from surgical intervention. Removal of the pituitary gland or the adrenal glands from rats that are normally resistant to inflammatory disease ren-

brain-immune communication system by inflammatory, toxic or infectious agents could contribute to some of the variations in the course of the immune system's inflammatory response.

CRH and Depression

ALTHOUGH THE ROLE of the stress response in inflammatory disease in humans is more difficult to prove, there is growing evidence that a wide variety of such diseases are associated with impairment of the HPA axis and lower levels of CRH secretion, which ultimately results in a hyperactive immune system. Furthermore, patients with a mood disorder called atypical depression also have a blunted stress response and impaired CRH function, which leads to lethargy, fatigue, increased sleep and increased eating that often results in weight gain.

Patients with other illnesses characterized by lethargy and fatigue, such as chronic fatigue syndrome, fibromyalgia and seasonal affective disorder (SAD), exhibit features of both depression and a hyperactive immune system. A person with chronic fatigue syndrome classically manifests debilitating lethargy or fatigue lasting six months or longer with no demonstrable medical cause, as well as feverishness, aches in joints and muscles, allergic symptoms and higher levels of antibodies to a variety of viral antigens (including Epstein-Barr virus).

Patients with fibromyalgia suffer from muscle aches, joint pains and sleep abnormalities, symptoms similar to early, mild rheumatoid arthritis. Both these illnesses are associated with a fatigue like that in atypical depression. SAD, which usually occurs in winter, is typified by lethargy, fatigue, increased food intake and increased sleep, symptoms similar to those of atypical depression.

A deficiency of CRH could contribute to lethargy in patients with chronic fatigue syndrome. Injection of CRH into these patients causes a delayed and blunted ACTH secretion by the HPA axis. That same response is also seen in patients whose hypothalamus has been injured or who have a tumor. Also, fatigue and hyperactivity of the immune response are associated with cortisol deficiency, which occurs when CRH secretion decreases. The hormone levels and responses in patients with fatigue syndromes suggest—but do not prove—that their HPA axis functions are impaired, resulting in a decrease in CRH and cortisol secretion and an increase in immune system activity. Together these findings indicate that human illness characterized by fatigue and hyperimmunity could possibly be treated by drugs that mimic CRH actions in the brain.

In contrast, the classic form of depression, melancholia, is actually not a state of inactivation and suppression of thought and feeling; rather it presents as an organized state of anxiety. The anxiety of melancholia is chiefly about the self. Melancholic patients feel impoverished and defective and often express hopelessness about the prospects for their unworthy selves in either love or work. The anxious hyperarousal of melancholic patients also manifests as a pervasive sense of vulnerability.

Melancholic patients also show behavioral alterations suggestive of physiological hyperarousal. They characteristically suffer from insomnia (usually early-morning awakening) and experience inhibition of eating, sexual activity and menstruation. One of the most widely found biological abnormalities in patients with melancholia is that of sustained hypersecretion of cortisol.

Many studies have been conducted on

INTERACTION OF THE BRAIN AND IMMUNE SYSTEM

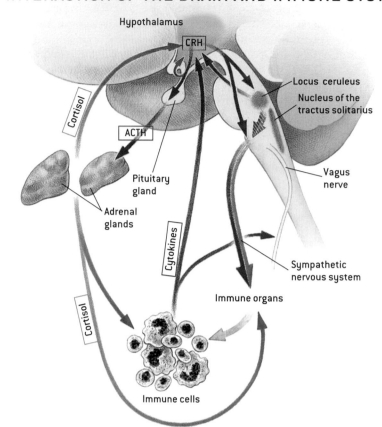

BRAIN AND IMMUNE SYSTEM can either stimulate (*red arrows*) or inhibit (*blue arrows*) each other. Immune cells produce cytokines (chemical signals) that stimulate the hypothalamus through the bloodstream or via nerves elsewhere in the body. The hormone CRH, produced in the hypothalamus, activates the HPA axis. The release of cortisol tunes down the immune system. CRH, acting on the brain stem, stimulates the sympathetic nervous system, which innervates immune organs and regulates inflammatory responses throughout the body. Disruption of these communications in any way leads to greater susceptibility to disease and immune complications.

patients with major depression to determine whether the excessive level of cortisol associated with depression correlates with suppressed immune responses. Some have found a correlation between hypercortisolism and immunosuppression; others have not. Because depression can have a variety of mental and biochemical causes, only some depressed patients may be immunosuppressed.

The excessive secretion of cortisol in melancholic patients is predominantly the result of hypersecretion of CRH, caused by a defect in or above the hypothalamus. Thus, the clinical and biochemical manifestations of melancholia reflect a generalized stress response that has escaped the usual counterregulation, remaining stuck in the "on" position.

The effects of tricyclic antidepressant drugs on components of the stress response support the concept that melancholia is associated with a chronic stress response. In rats, regular, but not acute, administration of the tricyclic antidepressant imipramine significantly lowers the levels of CRH precursors in the hypothalamus. Imipramine given for two months to healthy people with normal cortisol levels causes a gradual and sustained decrease in CRH secretion and other HPA axis functions, indicating that down-regulation of important components of the stress response is an intrinsic effect of imipramine.

Depression is also associated with inflammatory disease. About 20 percent of patients with rheumatoid arthritis develop clinical depression. A questionnaire commonly used by clinicians to diagnose depression contains about a dozen questions that are almost always answered affirmatively by patients with arthritis.

In the past, the association between an inflammatory disease and stress was considered by doctors to be secondary to the chronic pain and debilitation of the disease. The recent discovery of the common underpinning of the immune and stress responses may provide an explanation of why a patient can be susceptible to both inflammatory disease and depression. The hormonal dysregulation that underlies both inflammatory disease and depression can lead to either illness, depending on whether the perturbing stimulus is pro-inflammatory or psychologically stressful. That may explain why the waxing and waning of depression in arthritic patients does not always coincide with inflammatory flare-ups.

dividual's susceptibility to infectious diseases. The regulation of the immune system by the neurohormonal stress system provides a biological basis for understanding how stress might affect these diseases. Thus, stress hormones released from the brain, cortisol from the adrenal glands, and nerve chemicals released from nerve endings (adrenalinlike molecules norepinephrine and epinephrine) all modify the ability of immune cells to fight infectious agents and foreign molecules.

There is evidence that stress does affect human immune responses to viruses and bacteria. In studies with volunteers

es, such as herpes and influenza virus.

Animal studies provide further evidence that stress affects the course and severity of viral illness, bacterial disease and septic shock. Stress in mice worsens the severity of influenza infection through both the HPA axis and the sympathetic nervous system. Animal studies suggest that neuroendocrine mechanisms could play a similar role in infections with other viruses, including HIV, and provide a mechanism for understanding clinical observations that stress may exacerbate the course of AIDS. Stress, through cortisol, increases the susceptibility of mice to in-

Psychological STRESS CAN AFFECT an individual's SUSCEPTIBILITY to infectious diseases.

The popular belief that stress exacerbates inflammatory illness and that relaxation or removal of stress ameliorates it may indeed have a basis in fact. The interactions of the stress and immune systems and the hormonal responses they have in common could explain how conscious attempts to tone down responsivity to stress could affect immune responses.

Genetic Factors

HOW MUCH of the responsivity to stress is genetically determined and how much can be consciously controlled is not known. The set point of the stress response is to some extent genetically determined. In addition, factors in early development, learning, and later experiences contribute to differences in stress responsiveness. An event that is physiologically highly stressful to one individual may be much less so to another, depending on the sum of each person's genetic tendency to hormonal reactivity and their previous experience. The degree to which stress could precipitate or exacerbate disease would then depend not only on the intensity and duration of the stressful stimulus but also on the person's learned perception of the event as stressful and on the set point of the stress system.

Psychological stress can affect an in-

given a standard dose of the common cold virus (rhinovirus), individuals who are simultaneously exposed to stress show more viral particles and produce more mucus than do nonstressed individuals. Medical students receiving hepatitis vaccination during their final exams do not develop full protection against hepatitis. These findings have important implications for public health. People who are vaccinated during periods of stress might be less likely to develop full antibody protection. Chronic stress also prolongs wound healing.

New research shows that at physiological concentrations and under certain conditions the stress hormone cortisol not only is immunosuppressive but also may enhance certain aspects of immune function. Furthermore, each part of the stress response—the brain-hormonal, the adrenalinlike nerve and the adrenal gland adrenalin—is regulated independently, depending on the nature of the stressful stimulus. This specific nature of the stress response explains how different kinds and patterns of stress affect illness differently. Therefore, whereas chronic stress is generally immunosuppressive, acute stress can enhance cell-mediated immunity and exacerbate contact dermatitis types of allergic skin reactions. Furthermore, animal studies show that social stress and physical stress have different effects on infection with different virus-

fection with mycobacteria, the bacteria that causes tuberculosis. It has been shown that an intact HPA axis protects rats against the lethal septic effects of salmonella bacteria. Finally, new understanding of interactions of the immune and stress responses can help explain the puzzling observation that classic psychological conditioning of animals can influence their immune responses. For example, working with mice and rats, Robert Ader and Nicholas Cohen of the University of Rochester paired saccharin-flavored water with an immunosuppressive drug. Eventually the saccharin alone produced a decrease in immune function similar to that of the drug.

Social Stresses

STRESS NOT ONLY IS personal but is perceived through the prism of social interactions. These interactions can either add to or lessen psychological stress and affect our hormonal responses to it, which in turn can alter immune responses. Thus, the social-psychological stresses that we experience can affect our susceptibility to inflammatory and infectious diseases as well as the course of these and other diseases. For instance, in humans, loneliness is associated with a "threat," or adrenalinlike pattern of activation of the stress response and high blood pressure, whereas exercising is associated with a "challenge" pattern of high blood

IMMUNE SIGNALS TO THE BRAIN via the bloodstream can occur directly or indirectly. Immune cells such as monocytes, a type of white blood cell, produce a chemical messenger called interleukin-1 (IL-1), which ordinarily will not pass through the blood-brain barrier. But certain cerebral blood vessels contain leaky junctions, which allow IL-1 molecules to pass into the brain. There they can activate the HPA axis and other neural systems. IL-1 also binds to receptors on the endothelial cells that line cerebral blood vessels. This binding can cause enzymes in the cells to produce nitric oxide or prostaglandins, which diffuse into the brain and act directly on neurons.

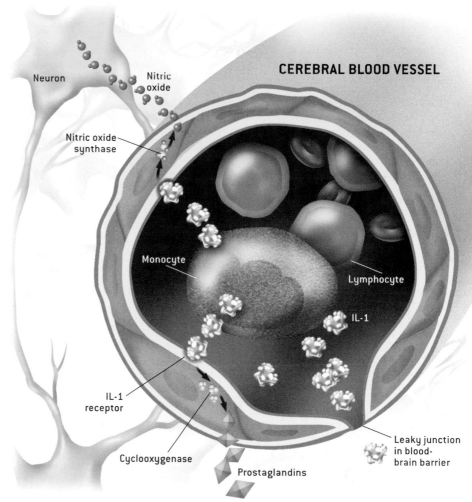

flow and cardiac output. Studies have shown that people exposed to chronic social stresses for more than two months have increased susceptibility to the common cold.

Other studies have shown that the immune responses of long-term caregivers, such as spouses of Alzheimer's patients, become blunted. Immune responses during marital discord are also blunted in the spouse (usually the wife) who experiences the greatest amount of stress and feelings of helplessness. In such a scenario, studies have found that the levels of stress hormones are elevated in the affected spouse.

On the other hand, a positive supportive environment of extensive social networks or group psychotherapy can enhance immune response and resistance to disease—even cancer. Some studies have shown that women with breast cancer, for instance, who receive strong, positive social support during their illness have significantly longer life spans than women without such support.

For centuries, taking the cure at a mountain sanatorium or a hot-springs spa was the only available treatment for many chronic diseases. New understanding of the communication between the brain and immune system provides a physiological explanation of why such cures sometimes worked. Disruption of this communication network leads to an increase in susceptibility to disease and can worsen the course of the illness. Restoration of this communication system, whether through pharmacological agents or the relaxing effects of a spa, can be the first step on the road to recovery.

A corollary of these findings is that psychoactive drugs may be used to treat some inflammatory diseases, and drugs that affect the immune system may be useful in treating some psychiatric disorders. There is growing evidence that our view of ourselves and others, our style of handling stresses, and our genetic makeup can affect the immune system. Similarly, there is good evidence that diseases associated with chronic inflammation significantly affect one's mood or level of anxiety. Finally, these findings suggest that classification of illnesses into medical and psychiatric specialties, and the boundaries that have demarcated mind and body, are artificial. SA

MORE TO EXPLORE

Measuring Stress: A Guide for Health and Social Scientists. Edited by Sheldon Cohen, Ronald C. Kessler and Lynn Underwood Gordon. Oxford University Press, 1998.

Why Zebras Don't Get Ulcers: An Updated Guide to Stress-Related Disease and Coping. Robert M. Sapolsky. W. H. Freeman and Company, 1998.

The Cell Biology of the Blood-Brain Barrier. L. L. Rubin and J. M. Staddon in *Annual Review of Neuroscience*, Vol. 22, pages 11–28; 1999.

The Biological Basis for Mind Body Interactions. Edited by E. A. Mayer and C. B. Saper. *Progress in Brain Research*, Vol. 122. Elsevier Science, 2000.

The Autonomic Nervous System in Health and Disease. David S. Goldstein. Marcel Dekker, 2001.

The Balance Within: The Science Connecting Health and Emotions. Esther M. Sternberg. Henry Holt and Company, 2000 (paperbound, 2001).

Science of Mind-Body: An Exploration of Integrative Mechanisms. Videocast of conference, National Institutes of Health, March 26–28, 2001. The videocast can be found online at http://videocast.nih.gov/PastEvents.asp?c+1&s+51

Neuroendocrine Regulation of Immunity. Jeanette I. Webster, Leonardo Tonelli and Esther M. Sternberg in *Annual Review of Immunology*, Vol. 20, pages 125–163; 2002.

Neural Immune Interactions in Health and Disease. Esther M. Sternberg and J. I. Webster in *Fundamental Immunology.* Fifth edition. Edited by William E. Paul. Lippincott Williams & Wilkins (forthcoming).

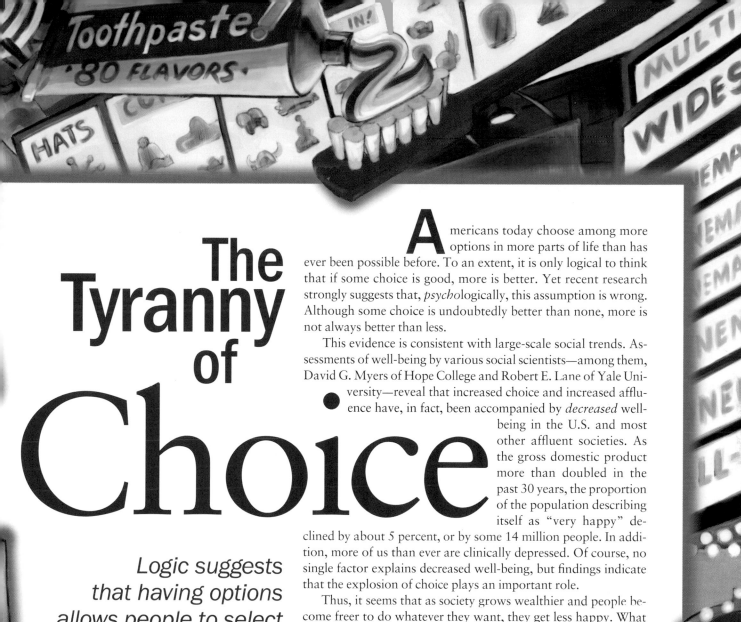

The Tyranny of Choice

Logic suggests that having options allows people to select precisely what makes them happiest. But, as studies show, abundant choice often makes for misery

By Barry Schwartz

Americans today choose among more options in more parts of life than has ever been possible before. To an extent, it is only logical to think that if some choice is good, more is better. Yet recent research strongly suggests that, *psycho*logically, this assumption is wrong. Although some choice is undoubtedly better than none, more is not always better than less.

This evidence is consistent with large-scale social trends. Assessments of well-being by various social scientists—among them, David G. Myers of Hope College and Robert E. Lane of Yale University—reveal that increased choice and increased affluence have, in fact, been accompanied by *decreased* well-being in the U.S. and most other affluent societies. As the gross domestic product more than doubled in the past 30 years, the proportion of the population describing itself as "very happy" declined by about 5 percent, or by some 14 million people. In addition, more of us than ever are clinically depressed. Of course, no single factor explains decreased well-being, but findings indicate that the explosion of choice plays an important role.

Thus, it seems that as society grows wealthier and people become freer to do whatever they want, they get less happy. What could account for this degree of misery?

Along with several colleagues, I have recently conducted research that offers insight into why many people end up unhappy rather than pleased when their options expand. We began by making a distinction between "maximizers" (those who always aim to make the best possible choice) and "satisficers" (those who aim for "good enough," whether or not better selections might be out there). We borrowed the term "satisficers" from the late Nobel Prize–winning psychologist and economist Herbert A. Simon of Carnegie Mellon University.

Next, we composed a set of statements—the Maximization Scale—to diagnose people's propensity to maximize. Then we had several thousand people rate themselves from 1 to 7 (from "completely disagree" to "completely agree") on such statements as "I never settle for second best." We also evaluated their sense of satisfaction with their decisions.

We did not define a sharp cutoff to separate maximizers from satisficers, but in general, we think of individuals whose average scores are higher than 4 (the scale's midpoint) as maximizers and those whose scores are lower

(The Maximization Scale)

The statements below distinguish maximizers from satisficers. Subjects rate themselves from 1 to 7, from "completely disagree" to "completely agree," on each statement. Analysts generally consider people whose average rating is higher than 4 to be maximizers. When we looked at averages from thousands of subjects, we found that about a third scored higher than 4.75 and a third lower than 3.25. Roughly 10 percent of subjects were extreme maximizers (averaging greater than 5.5), and 10 percent were extreme satisficers (averaging lower than 2.5). —*B.S.*

1 **Whenever I'm faced with a choice, I try to imagine what all the other possibilities are, even ones that aren't present at the moment.**

2 **No matter how satisfied I am with my job, it's only right for me to be on the lookout for better opportunities.**

3 **When I am in the car listening to the radio, I often check other stations to see if something better is playing, even if I am relatively satisfied with what I'm listening to.**

4 **When I watch TV, I channel surf, often scanning through the available options even while attempting to watch one program.**

5 **I treat relationships like clothing: I expect to try a lot on before finding the perfect fit.**

6 **I often find it difficult to shop for a gift for a friend.**

7 **Renting videos is really difficult. I'm always struggling to pick the best one.**

8 **When shopping, I have a hard time finding clothing that I really love.**

9 **I'm a big fan of lists that attempt to rank things (the best movies, the best singers, the best athletes, the best novels, etc.).**

10 **I find that writing is very difficult, even if it's just writing a letter to a friend, because it's so hard to word things just right. I often do several drafts of even simple things.**

11 **No matter what I do, I have the highest standards for myself.**

12 **I never settle for second best.**

13 **I often fantasize about living in ways that are quite different from my actual life.**

than the midpoint as satisficers. People who score highest on the test—the greatest maximizers—engage in more product comparisons than the lowest scorers, both before and after they make purchasing decisions, and they take longer to decide what to buy. When satisficers find an item that meets their standards, they stop looking. But maximizers exert enormous effort reading labels, checking out consumer magazines and trying new products. They also spend more time comparing their purchasing decisions with those of others.

Naturally, no one can check out every option, but maximizers strive toward that goal, and so making a decision becomes increasingly daunting as the number of choices rises. Worse, after making a selection, they are nagged by the alternatives they have not had time to investigate. In the end, they are more likely to make better objective choices than satisficers but get less satisfaction from them. When reality requires maximizers to compromise—to end a search and decide on something—apprehension about what might have been takes over.

We found as well that the greatest maximizers are the least happy with the fruits of their efforts. When they compare themselves with others, they get little pleasure from finding out that they did better and substantial dissatisfaction from finding out that they did worse. They are more prone to experiencing regret after a purchase, and if their acquisition disappoints them, their sense of well-being takes longer to recover. They also tend to brood or ruminate more than satisficers do. Working with Columbia University psychologists Rachael F. Elwork and Sheena S. Iyengar, I found that maximizing college seniors searching for jobs actually found positions with 20 percent higher starting salaries than satisficing job seekers. Yet the maximizers were less satisfied with the jobs they got, and with the entire search process, than the satisficers were.

Does it follow that maximizers are less happy in general than satisficers? I and other researchers tested this by having people fill out a variety of questionnaires known to be reliable indicators of well-being. As might be expected, individuals with high maximization scores experienced less satisfaction with life and were less happy, less optimistic and more depressed than people with low maximization scores. Indeed, those with extreme maximization ratings had depression scores that placed them in the borderline clinical range.

Recipe for Unhappiness

Several factors explain why more choice is not always better than less, especially for maximizers. High among these are "opportunity costs." The quality of any given option cannot be assessed in isolation from its alternatives. One of the "costs" of making a selection is losing the opportunities that a different option would have afforded. Thus, an opportunity cost of vacationing on the beach in Cape Cod might be missing the fabulous restaurants in the Napa Valley. If we assume that opportunity costs reduce the overall desirability of the most preferred choice, then the more alternatives there are, the deeper our sense of loss will be and the less satisfaction we will derive from our ultimate decision. Lyle Brenner of the University of Florida and his

Feelings Evoked by Ever More Choices

E arly research showed that people respond more strongly to losses than gains (*left graph*). Similarly, feelings of well-being initially rise as choice increases (*blue line in center graph*) but then level off quickly (good feelings satiate). Meanwhile, although zero choice (*at the* y *axis*) evokes virtually infinite unhappiness, bad feelings escalate (*red line*) as we go from having few choices to many. The net result (*purple line in right graph*) is that, at some point, added choice only decreases happiness. —B.S.

REACTIONS TO LOSSES AND GAINS

REACTIONS TO INCREASING CHOICE

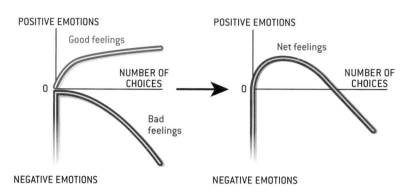

collaborators demonstrated the effects of opportunity costs when they had subjects put a dollar value on subscriptions to magazines or flights from San Francisco. Some attached prices to a single magazine subscription or a single destination. Others attached prices to the same magazine or destination when it was part of a group containing three others. Prices were consistently lower when a given alternative was evaluated as part of a group than when it was evaluated in isolation.

Why might this be so? When you assign a value to, say, *Newsweek*, as part of a group that also contains *People* and *Us*, your tendency will be to compare the magazines. Each comparison that *Newsweek* wins will be a gain, but each comparison that it loses will be a loss, an opportunity cost. But we know from the research of Nobelist psychologist Daniel Kahneman of Princeton University and his late colleague Amos Tversky of Stanford that losses (in this case, opportunity costs) have a much greater psychological impact than gains. Losses make us hurt more than gains make us feel good.

Sometimes opportunity costs may create enough conflict to produce paralysis. The problem of opportunity costs will be worse for a maximizer than for a satisficer. The latter's "good enough" philosophy can survive thoughts about opportunity costs. The "good enough" standard also leads to much less searching and inspection of alternatives than the maximizer's "best" standard. With fewer choices under consideration, a person will have fewer opportunity costs to subtract.

Regret Adds to Costs

Just as people feel sorrow about the opportunities they have forgone, they may also suffer regret about the option they settle on. My colleagues and I devised a scale to measure proneness to feeling regret and found that people with high sensitivity to regret are less happy, less satisfied with life, less optimistic and more depressed than those with low sensitivity. Not surprisingly, we also found that people with high regret sensitivity tend to be maximizers. We think that worry over future regret is a major reason that individuals become maximizers. The only way to be sure you will not regret a decision is by making the best possible one.

Regret may be one reason for our aversion to losses. Have you ever bought an expensive pair of shoes only to discover that they are so uncomfortable that you cannot wear them for more than 10 minutes without hobbling? Did you toss them out, or are they still sitting in the back of your closet? Chances are you had a hard time throwing them away. Having bought the shoes, you incurred an actual, or "sunk," cost, and you are going to keep them around in the hope that eventually you will get your money's worth out of them. To give the shoes away or throw them out would force you to acknowledge a mistake—a loss.

In a classic demonstration of the power of sunk costs, people were offered season subscriptions to a local theater company. Some were offered the tickets at full price and others at a discount. Then the researchers timed how often the purchasers attended

Lessons

Choose when to choose.
We can decide to restrict our options when the decision is not crucial. For example, make a rule to visit no more than two stores when shopping for clothing.

Learn to accept "good enough."
Settle for a choice that meets your core requirements rather than searching for the elusive "best." Then stop thinking about it.

Don't worry about what you're missing.
Consciously limit how much you ponder the seemingly attractive features of options you reject. Teach yourself to focus on the positive parts of the selection you make.

Control expectations.
"Don't expect too much, and you won't be disappointed" is a cliché but can help you be more satisfied with life. —B.S.

the plays. Full-price payers were more likely to show up than discount payers. The reason for this, the investigators argued, was that the full-price payers would experience more regret if they did not use the tickets because that would constitute a bigger loss.

Several studies have shown that two of the factors affecting regret are how much personal responsibility one feels for the result and how easy it is to imagine a better alternative. The availability of choice obviously exacerbates both these factors. When you have no options, what can you do? You will feel disappointment, maybe; regret, no. But with many options, the chances increase that a really good one is out there, and you may well feel that you ought to have been able to find it.

Adaptation Dulls Joy

A phenomenon called adaptation also contributes to the fallout we face from too many choices. Simply put, we get used to things, and as a result, very little in life turns out quite as good as we expect it to be. After much anguish, you might decide to buy a certain luxury car and then try to put

(The Author)

BARRY SCHWARTZ is Dorwin Cartwright Professor of Social Theory and Social Action in the department of psychology at Swarthmore College, where he has taught since 1971. He recently published a book on the consequences of excessive choice [see "Further Reading," on opposite page] and has written several other books, including *The Battle for Human Nature* and *The Costs of Living*.

all the attractions of other models out of your mind. But once you are driving your car, adaptation begins, and the experience falls just a little bit flat. You are hit with a double whammy—regret about what you did not choose and disappointment with what you did, even if your decision was not bad.

Because of adaptation, enthusiasm about positive experiences does not sustain itself. Daniel T. Gilbert of Harvard University and Timothy D. Wilson of the University of Virginia have shown that people consistently mispredict how long good experiences will make them feel good and how long bad experiences will make them feel bad. The waning of pleasure or enjoyment over time always seems to come as an unpleasant surprise.

And it may cause more disappointment in a world of many options. The opportunity costs associated with a decision and the time and effort that go into making it are "fixed costs" that we "pay" up front, and those costs then get "amortized" over the life of the decision. The more we invest in a decision, the more satisfaction we expect to realize from our investment. If the decision provides substantial satisfaction for a long time after it is made, the costs of making it recede into insignificance. But if the decision provides pleasure for only a short time, those costs loom large. Spending four months deciding what stereo to buy is not so bad if you really enjoy that stereo for 15 years. But if you are excited by it for six months and then adapt, you may feel like a fool for having put in all that effort.

The Curse of High Expectations

A surfeit of alternatives can cause distress in yet another way: by raising expectations. In the fall of 1999 the *New York Times* and CBS News asked teenagers to compare their experiences with those their parents had growing up. Fifty percent of children from affluent households said their lives were harder. When questioned further, these adolescents talked about high expectations, both their own and their parents'. They talked about "too muchness": too many activities, too many consumer choices, too much to learn. As one commentator put it, "Children feel the pressure ... to be sure they don't slide back. Everything's about going forward.... Falling back is the American nightmare." So if your perch is high, you have much further to fall than if your perch is low.

The amount of choice we now have in most aspects of our lives contributes to high expectations. When I was on vacation a few years ago in a tiny seaside town on the Oregon coast, I went into the local grocery store to buy ingredients for dinner. The store offered about a dozen options for wine. What I got was so-so, but I did not expect to be able to get something very good and, hence, was satisfied with what I had. If instead I had been shopping in a store that offered an abundance of choices, my expectations would have been a good deal higher and even a better wine might have left me sorely disappointed. When we say an experience was good, what we mean, in part, is that it was better than we expected it to be. High expectations almost guarantee that experiences will fall short, especially for maximizers and especially when regret, opportunity costs and adaptation do not factor into our expectations.

A Link to Depression?

The consequences of unlimited choice may go far beyond mild disappointment. Americans are showing a decrease in happiness and an increase in clinical depression. One important contributing factor is that when we make decisions, experience the consequences and find that they do not live up to expectations, we blame ourselves. Disappointing outcomes constitute personal failures.

The research that my colleagues and I have done suggests that maximizers are prime candidates for depression. With group after group of people, varying in age (including young adolescents), gender, educational level, geographic location, race and socioeconomic status, we have found a strong correlation between maximizing and measures of depression. If the experience of disappointment is relentless, if virtually every choice you make fails to live up to expectations and aspirations, and if you consistently take personal responsibility for the disappointments, then the trivial looms larger and larger, and the conclusion that you cannot do anything right becomes devastating. Although depression has many sources, and the relation among choice, maximizing and depression requires more study, there is good reason to believe that overwhelming choice at least contributes to the epidemic of unhappiness spreading through modern society.

What Can Be Done

The news I have reported is not good. Does it mean that we would all be better off if our choices were severely restricted, even eliminated? I do not think so. The relation between choice and well-being is complicated. Being able to choose has enormously important positive effects on us. But only up to a point. As the number of choices we face increases, the psychological benefits we derive start to level off. And some of the negative effects of choice accelerate. A quarter of a century ago the late Clyde H. Coombs of the University of Michigan at Ann Arbor and George S. Avrunin of the Universi-

ty of Massachusetts at Amherst noted that good feelings "satiate" and bad feelings "escalate." Much the same can be said of choice: what is good about choice "satiates" and what is bad about it "escalates." A point is reached at which increased choice brings increased misery. It appears that American society has long since passed that point.

Few Americans would favor passing laws to limit choices. But individuals can certainly take steps to mitigate choice-related distress. Such actions require practice, discipline and perhaps a new way of thinking, but each should bring its own rewards [see box on opposite page].

Beyond those individual strategies, our society would be well served to rethink its worship of choice. As I write this, public debate continues about privatization of Social Security (so people could select their retirement investments), privatization of Medicare and prescription drug benefits (so people could choose their own health plans), and choice in public education. And everyone seems to insist that having patients choose their treatments will make them better off. Software developers design their products so that users can customize them to their own specific needs and tastes, as if the resulting complexity and confusion are worth it. Manufacturers keep offering new versions of old products, as if we needed more variety. The lesson is that developments in each of these spheres may well rest on assumptions that are deeply mistaken.

(Further Reading)

- **The American Paradox: Spiritual Hunger in an Age of Plenty.** David Myers. Yale University Press, 2001.
- **The Loss of Happiness in Market Democracies.** Robert E. Lane. Yale University Press, 2001.
- **Maximizing versus Satisficing: Happiness Is a Matter of Choice.** Barry Schwartz et al. in *Journal of Personality and Social Psychology,* Vol. 83, No. 5, pages 1178–1197; 2002.
- **The Paradox of Choice: Why More Is Less.** Barry Schwartz. Ecco/HarperCollins Publishers, 2004.

Depressingly Easy

We nuke prepared dishes rather than growing our own food and machine-wash ready-made clothes rather than sewing and scrubbing. Such conveniences may be contributing to rising rates of depression by depriving our brains of their hard-earned rewards By Kelly Lambert

For several decades, the multibillion-dollar antidepressant industry has pointed to imbalances in the neurochemical serotonin as the cause of depression. But research has yet to find convincing evidence that serotonin imbalances represent the indisputable cause of depression, and despite the unprecedented number of pharmacological treatment options available today, depression rates are higher than ever.

If Big Pharma does not have a cure for depression, shouldn't we pursue a fresh approach to this vexing problem? Could there be a nonpharmacological treatment strategy that would bring relief to the increasing number of people struggling with this mood disorder, for instance? What do we know about how to preserve good mental health? Is it possible to maintain a sense of control over our increasingly stressful daily lives, so that we can refocus our attention on more meaningful psychological endeavors, such as the challenging issues of problem solving and planning for our futures?

Is there something about how we live today that's actually toxic to our mental health? Were earlier generations somehow less susceptible to depressive symptoms? If so, what can we learn from how they lived that will help us rebuild our resilience and emotional well-being? To build a new, more integrated theory of depression, I have searched the literature for possible evolutionary triggers of emotional responses, reevaluated what we know about how the brain functions in both healthy and unhealthy ways, and identified pivotal lifestyle factors that might be affecting our society adversely.

I began thinking about the impact our contemporary lifestyle has on our mental health more than 10 years ago, after attending a lecture by Martin Seligman, a psychologist and the pioneering creator of the Positive Psychology movement, who was then president of the American Psychological Association. Seligman described two studies conducted in the 1970s in which people in different age groups were questioned about bouts of depression they had experienced during their lifetimes. The researchers then compared the responses of different generations.

The result should be a no-brainer, I thought at the time. Of course, older people would report more bouts of depression. After all, they had lived through the Great Depression and two world wars and suffered far more hardships and loss just by virtue of having lived longer. How could their mental anguish compare with the shorter (so far), easier and much less traumatic lives of a younger generation?

To my surprise, the exact opposite was true. Seligman reported that younger people were much more likely to have experienced depression. In fact, one study found that those born in the middle third of the 20th century were 10 times more likely to suffer from major depression than those born in the first third of the century were. These findings were later corroborated in a second study.

What is behind this startling disparity? For one thing, earlier generations did far more phys-ical work than we do today. I was reminded of just how much our daily lives have changed six years ago, while reading a bedtime story to my younger daughter, who was three at the time. Skylar had chosen *Little House on the Prairie* for that evening—one of my childhood favorites.

Yesterday and Today

Over the years as I've read to my daughters I've often used the time to think through my to-do list for the next day. This bit of cognitive multitasking was a piece of cake with books such as *Goodnight Moon,* which I had read countless times when my girls were younger. "Goodnight room".... I need to update that section in Wednesday's lecture. "Goodnight moon".... and remember to take the chicken breasts out of the freezer. "Goodnight cow jumping over the moon".... I have to finish those analyses of the rat brains in the lab tomorrow. "Goodnight light".... I need to sign that permission slip for my older daughter Lara's field trip.

But that night the story about life on the prairie somehow drew me in. I found the demanding lives of Ma and Pa Ingalls so compelling that I actually had to pay attention! Laura Ingalls Wilder, their daughter, described in detail how the family planted, harvested and hunted down all their food throughout the year. That made my trips to the supermarket and merely reading the heating instructions for much of the food I "prepared" seem, well, lame.

I had always complained about doing laundry, but my efforts paled in comparison to those of Ma Ingalls. She had to scrub every garment on a washboard and then hang the clothes out to dry. And she had made all the garments with her own hands! Bathing my daughters did not require collecting rainwater or drawing water from a well; I merely had to turn on a faucet. The Ingalls family had to make most of the things I simply purchased, including toys, candles, soap, honey and butter. *Little House* crashed this working mom's self-pity party that evening. My life is a walk in the park compared with the lifestyles of a century earlier, I realized.

Clearly, I'm not suggesting that we go back to churning butter and tanning hides. But I do think we have to examine whether our cushy, digitally driven contemporary lifestyles—replete with SUVs, DVDs, laptops, cell phones and, yes, microwave ovens—may be at the root of the soaring

---

FAST FACTS
The Mental Perils of Ease

1》 Rates of depression have risen in recent decades, at the same time that people are enjoying time-saving conveniences such as microwave ovens, e-mail, prepared meals, and machines for washing clothes and mowing lawns.

2》 People of earlier generations, whose lives were characterized by greater efforts just to survive, paradoxically, were mentally healthier. Human ancestors also evolved in conditions where hard physical work was necessary to thrive.

3》 By denying our brains the rewards that come from anticipating and executing complex tasks with our hands, the author argues, we undercut our mental well-being.

pushing buttons instead of plowing fields?

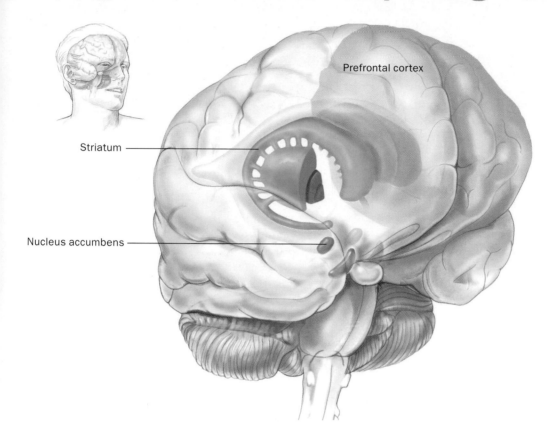

Striatum

Nucleus accumbens

Prefrontal cortex

The nucleus accumbens, the brain's pleasure center, forms a critical interface between the motor system, or striatum, and the prefrontal cortex, which controls thought processes.

rates of depression in people born in the latter part of the 20th century. Did we lose something vital to our mental health when we started pushing buttons instead of plowing fields? From a neuroanatomical point of view, I believe the answer is an emphatic yes.

Will Work for Pleasure

Our brains are programmed to derive a deep sense of satisfaction and pleasure when our physical effort produces something tangible, visible and—this fact is extremely important—meaningful in gaining the resources necessary for survival. In fact, our brains have been hardwired for this type of meaningful action since our ancestors were dressed in pelts. After all, nature needed a way to keep the earliest humans from becoming "cave potatoes." Hanging out all day didn't put freshly caught game on the campfire or help maintain a safe place to live.

I call this emotional payoff "effort-driven rewards." There are other important benefits to this type of effort beyond a greater sense of psychological well-being. We also experience an increased perception of control over our environment, more positive emotions and, perhaps most

critical, enhanced resilience against mental illnesses such as depression.

Think about effort-driven rewards as a clever evolutionary tool, a way to motivate early humans to maintain the physical activity needed to obtain the resources to live—to find food, protect themselves from the elements and procreate to continue the species. Effort-driven rewards don't come just from physical effort, however. They also involve complex movement coupled with intricate thought processes. Imagine thousands of years ago, when our ancestors were tracking a pack of wild boars through a forest or across a plain. Because these animals are such vicious fighters, a successful strategy typically involved the coordinated efforts of a few hunters, requiring effective social communication and support. They needed to be wily as they chased their game or lured their prey into a trap that they had built. All their efforts were fueled by anticipation. In fact, anticipating something pleasurable creates more activity in the pleasure center of the brain than actually achieving the goal does. Once they caught their prey, our hunters were suffused with a sense of accomplishment and satisfaction as they skinned the animal before dinner.

Our hands play a crucial role when it comes to effort-driven rewards. From an evolutionary perspective, it is easy to see why they have always been so critical to our survival: they allow us to gain control of our environment. In fact, an essential premise of the proposed effort-driven-rewards theory is that movement—and especially hand movements that lead to desired outcomes—plays a key role in both preventing the onset of and building resilience against depression and other emotional disorders. Furthermore, we are predisposed to preferring hand movements that our ancestors needed for survival—those necessary for nurturing, cleaning, cooking, grooming, building shelter and farming.

But these days we shop at Whole Foods and drive Hummers. What does all this history have to do with our modern lives and depression? Our brains are generally the same size and have all the same parts and chemical composition as those of the earliest humans. Even though our lifestyles have changed radically, we have retained the in-

nate need for achieving effort-driven rewards.

Is it okay that we have systematically removed physical effort—and all the complexity of movement and thought processes that it implies—from effort-driven rewards? Is contemporary society actually robbing us of certain forms of pleasure so fundamental to our mental health?

How Our Brains Reward Effort

As I looked for the possible evolutionary triggers of depression, I also began to reexamine the primary symptoms. Over the past few decades researchers have identified certain areas of the brain associated with some of these symptoms. But could I match every single one—including loss of pleasure, feelings of worthlessness, slowed motor abilities and difficulty concentrating—to a specific part of the brain? And, significantly, were those different brain areas interconnected or linked in some clearly identifiable way?

A natural place to start was the nucleus accumbens. This peanut-size structure is known as

 The more the effort-driven-rewards system is

Hard work with hands is a likely factor in keeping the rate of depression in Amish communities far lower than it is in the rest of the U.S.

"Working rats" that had to search for hidden cereal learned to be persistent (*left*), which helped them solve new challenges; in contrast, "trust fund rats," which did not have to work for treats, gave up more easily (*right*).

the pleasure, or reward, center of the brain, and it keeps us engaged in behaviors that are important to our survival, including eating and having sex. It plays a crucial role in how the brain functions, as it determines how to respond to environmental stimuli such as a piece of chocolate cake or that handsome guy at the bar.

An integrating center of the brain, it receives inputs and outputs from many neural areas. But cortical area of our brain that controls higher thought processes. Because of the interconnectivity of the brain areas that control movement, emotion and thinking, doing activities that involve a number of these components fully engages the effort-driven-rewards circuit.

In fact, the more the effort-driven-rewards circuit is kept activated and humming, the greater the sense of psychological well-being that re-

humming, the greater the sense of well-being.

for our purposes, I am focusing on its intimate connection to three other primary areas. The accumbens is positioned in proximity to the brain's motor system, or striatum, which controls our movements, and the limbic system, a collection of structures involved in emotion and learning. Essentially, the accumbens is a critical interface between our emotions and our actions. The closely linked motor and emotional systems also extend to the prefrontal cortex, which controls our thought processes, including problem solving, planning and decision making.

It is this accumbens-striatal-cortical network—the crucial system that connects movement, emotion and thinking—that I call the effort-driven-rewards circuit. It is the proposed neuroanatomical network underlying the symptoms associated with depression. In fact, it is possible to correlate every symptom of depression with a brain part on this circuit. Loss of pleasure? The nucleus accumbens. Sluggishness and slow motor responses? The striatum. Negative feelings? The limbic system. Poor concentration? The prefrontal cortex.

As if to impart renewed energy to our behavior, the motor structures that control our movements are intimately connected to the reward center—where we register pleasure—and to the

sults. It is as if an electric current is coursing through the network. When it is buzzing at top capacity—when, for example, installing that new light fixture requires both hands—the cells in those areas of the brain are turned on and secreting neurochemicals, such as dopamine and serotonin, which are involved in generating positive emotions. Neural connections are strengthened and reinforced. Perhaps most important, this kind of meaningful action—that is, effort-driven rewards—likely stimulates neurogenesis, the production of new brain cells. Neurogenesis is believed to be an important factor in recovering from depression.

Our hands play a crucial role. They occupy most of the real estate of the motor cortex, located in the higher cortex (the brain's outer covering). In fact, our hands are so important that moving them activates larger areas of the brain's complex cortex than does moving much larger parts of our bodies, such as our backs or even our legs.

(The Author)

Neuroscientist and psychologist KELLY LAMBERT (www.kellylambert.com) is chair of psychology at Randolph-Macon College.

MOLLY HYER

rodents—in each mound. We trained the rats to search the mounds for the treat, and each day we changed the positions of the mounds randomly. The animals soon learned that each new mound had a Froot Loop, so once they retrieved one prize they moved on to the next mound. I designed this task to mimic "harvesting"—picking fruit, vegetables or, in this case, Froot Loops from the "fields."

Within a few days the rats immediately approached the mounds and started digging for their prized cereal pieces. We trained these rats every day for five weeks so they would have ample opportunities to make associations between their physical effort and desired rewards.

Our control group consisted of rats that we also placed in this novel environment every day. But regardless of the physical effort they exerted, they received their Froot Loop rewards in a lump sum in the corner of the apparatus. My students enjoyed calling these rats the "trust fund rats" and the digging rats the "working rats."

In the next phase, we developed a puzzle that the rats had to learn to solve. We wanted to assess whether the worker rats or the trust fund rats were more persistent in problem solving. We put a Froot Loop in a plastic cat-toy ball, a novel toy stimulus that would be mildly threatening to the animals because it had a bell in it. We made certain that the coveted cereal piece would not fit

Doing activities you find meaningful boosts

Knitting a sweater or cropping images into shape for a scrapbook project can alleviate stress and engage the brain in ways that benefit mental health.

As I continued to delve into the scientific research on depression, I found myself thinking more and more about the role of hands-on work and effort-driven rewards in our mental lives. Could adding simple tasks to our daily repertoire of activities help maintain emotional resilience? For the answer, there was just one place to go—back to the laboratory.

The Trust Fund Rats

Because the rat brain has all the same parts as the human brain (it is just smaller and less complex), rodent models are a great starting place for mental health research. Could the rats tell me if there was anything to the connection between depression and physical effort?

Two undergraduate students, Kelly Tu and Ashley Everette, helped me design a study to test my theory. We put four mounds of cage bedding in the testing apparatus and buried a Froot Loop—a culinary favorite among my laboratory

through the openings. That meant that no matter how clever or bold the rat was, it would not be able to retrieve the reward in the test's three-minute time frame. Of course, the rats would not know this factor, so we could assess the amount of time they spent trying to get the treat. The task involved boldness and persistence—characteristics that serve us all well during challenging times.

To make this task official, Craig Kinsley, my colleague from the University of Richmond who collaborated on this project, suggested we call it the "novel manipulandum task." This sounded much more impressive than the "cat-toy test."

What did we find? Although we made sure that both groups had equivalent levels of "emotionality," or anxiety, before training began, we observed remarkable differences in how the animals approached the challenge task. The worker rats picked up the ball in their mouths and slung their heads from side to side, tossing the ball across the cage. They also tried to stick their tiny paws through the openings to obtain the reward. Although the trust funders were just as motivated to retrieve the Froot Loop (both groups were on the same food-restriction regime) and used similar strategies, they were not nearly as persistent.

In fact, the worker rats spent approximately 60 percent more time trying to obtain the Froot Loop reward and made 30 percent more attempts to do so than the control group did. In their own way, the worker rats were telling us that their prior training sessions had made them more confident that they could overcome the challenge and retrieve the reward.

As I considered these findings, I was reminded of the widely reported study conducted several decades ago by Seligman and his colleague, psychologist Steven F. Maier of the University of Colorado at Boulder. In this famous experiment, dogs gave up responding and problem solving after they realized they could not escape from cages in which they received mild shocks. The researchers referred to this effort-consequence disconnect as "learned helplessness." Could our findings, then, be called "learned persistence"?

Clearly, we had empirical evidence of the adaptive value of effort-based rewards. The simple behavior of digging in mounds of bedding for cereal rewards had given the rats the motivation

rewards activate the problem-solving prefrontal cortex plus the movement-controlling striatum and the reward/motivation center known as the accumbens, leaving you with a fuller brain experience that prepares you for life's next challenge. The decreased brain activation associated with increasingly effortless-driven rewards may, over time, diminish your perception of control over your environment and increase your vulnerability to mental illnesses such as depression.

What can we do to protect ourselves against the onset or tenacious persistence of depression? Poring over a scrapbook project or knitting a sweater may distract you from the stress in your life and engage your brain in intense ways that are beneficial to your mental health. Going out to the park or gym to exercise, especially if you perceive the activity as meaningful, can also boost important, emotionally relevant neurochemicals such as serotonin and endorphins. Such activities may alter the brain in more meaningful ways than any dose of a single drug could accomplish. Why? Because they are performed within the context of your life. When you are faced with a challenge and embark on the dynamic process of deciding on an effective strategy, implementing the plan and observing the final desirable outcome, your brain takes note of these situations so that it can access similar response strategies in the future.

mportant, emotionally relevant neurochemicals.

and confidence to persevere on a completely different challenging task.

The Lifestyle-Depression Link

Even though our nervous systems have the same anatomical makeup and chemical composition as those of our ancestors—or even people who lived a mere century ago—we are clearly using our brains and our hands differently. The percentage of farmers in the workforce was 38 percent at the start of the 20th century but less than 3 percent at its end. Today many more of us are knowledge workers than physical laborers. There have been vast increases in service-related jobs, from 31 percent of the workforce in 1900 to 78 percent of all workers in 1999.

Of course, you may feel a sense of accomplishment when you zip through your cognitive to-do list. The pleasure derived from just intellectualizing a problem is rewarding because it activates the prefrontal cortex. But effort-driven

Just as a gymnast needs to complete simple muscle repetitions before she can learn complex routines, we need ongoing, positive experience with simple effort-driven rewards to execute the complex mental gymnastics that enrich our mental lives. Anything that lets us see a clear connection between effort and consequence—and that helps us feel in control of a challenging situation—is a kind of mental vitamin that helps build resilience and provides a buffer against depression. **M**

(Further Reading)

◆ **Increasing Rates of Depression.** G. L. Klerman and M. M. Weissman in *Journal of the American Medical Association*, Vol. 261, No. 15, pages 2229–2235; April 21, 1989.
◆ **Learned Optimism: How to Change Your Mind and Your Life.** Martin E. P. Seligman. Pocket Books, 1992.
◆ **Rising Rates of Depression in Today's Society: Consideration for the Roles of Effort-Based Rewards and Enhanced Resilience in Day-to-Day Functioning.** Kelly G. Lambert in *Neuroscience and Biobehavioral Reviews*, Vol. 30, No. 4, pages 497–510; 2006.

Psychotherapy on Trial

In the past half a century psychotherapy research has blossomed, with thousands of studies confirming its positive effects for a wide array of clinical problems, including depression, anxiety, eating disorders and sexual dysfunction. Yet in recent years, intense controversy over whether and how to put these findings into practice has erupted, further widening the "scientist-practitioner gap," the deep gulf that has separated many researchers and psychotherapists for decades.

The current debate centers on the growing use of empirically supported therapies, or ESTs, which are specific therapies for specific problems—for example, depression

© ANDY WARHOL FOUNDATION Corbis

→ **Empirically supported therapies seek to bring the power of research-proven techniques to the therapist's office. So why are they controversial?**
By Hal Arkowitz and Scott O. Lilienfeld

and bulimia—that meet certain criteria (such as a given number of well-designed studies showing positive effects) for treatment efficacy. Proponents have welcomed ESTs for their clear guidelines on what works for patients and their explicit manuals prescribing administration of treatment. Critics have sharply questioned ESTs on a number of grounds, namely, whether their research base is adequate, whether their one-size-fits-all approach can address the needs of individual patients, and whether their focus should be primarily alleviation of symptomatic distress or changes in underlying dispositions and vulnerabilities.

The debate's resolution bears important implications for treatments that psychotherapy patients seek and receive. A survey of nearly 10,000 adults published in 2005 showed that one out of four Americans meets the criteria for a diagnosis of a psychological disorder in any given year and

that slightly less than half of all people in the U.S. will suffer from a psychological disorder over the course of their lifetimes [see "Half Are Mentally Ill," by Jamie Talan, Head Lines; *Scientific American Mind*, Vol. 16, No. 3; 2005].

Before we wrote this article, one of us (Arkowitz) had been highly critical of ESTs (though not of placing psychotherapy on a more scientific basis). The other one of us (Lilienfeld) had been a strong advocate of ESTs. Ultimately we found considerable common ground on many points regarding the proper role of research in informing clinical practice. In this feature, we hope to offer a modest step toward reconciling opposing views on ESTs.

Laying the Groundwork

Fifty years ago the foundations of modern psychotherapy research were just being laid. One

How We Can Be Fooled

A variety of factors can lead unwary clinicians and researchers to conclude that a useless psychotherapy is in fact effective. These factors help to explain why psychotherapy research is necessary.

Spontaneous remission	Some psychotherapy clients may become better on their own
Placebo effects	Improvement results from the mere expectation of improvement
Regression to the mean	Extreme scores tend to become less extreme over time
Initial misdiagnosis	Some clients diagnosed with a mental disorder may either have no disorder at all or have a milder disorder
Multiple-treatment interference	Clients often obtain other types of treatment at the same time
Demand characteristics	Some clients may report what they believe their therapists want to hear, resulting in overly positive reports of improvement
Selective attrition	Clients who do not benefit from treatment may tend to drop out of psychotherapy, leaving only those clients who do benefit
Effort justification	Clients may feel a need to rationalize the time, energy and money they have expended in psychotherapy

participant at a 1950 conference was being only partially facetious when he commented: "Psychotherapy is an undefined technique applied to unspecified problems with unpredictable outcomes. For this technique we recommend rigorous training."

Just two years later an eminent British psychologist named Hans Eysenck questioned the scientific basis of talk therapy in a landmark paper—asserting that it was no more effective than the absence of treatment. Researchers soon rose to Eysenck's challenge, and thousands of studies over the ensuing decades demonstrated conclusively that psychotherapy does help many patients. But which are the most effective therapies and for which problems? Further studies sought answers.

In 1995 a task force of a division of the American Psychological Association (APA), chaired by Boston University psychologist Da-

vid H. Barlow, issued the first of several reports that set forth initial criteria for ESTs, along with lists of therapies that met those criteria. The current task force list is widely used today, especially in university settings in which future clinical psychologists are educated [*see box on page 109*].

We should note that the list tells only whether a treatment has been found to work in controlled studies but not necessarily in clinical practice outside the laboratory. Most experiments have examined cognitive-behavioral therapy; psychoanalytic, humanistic and integrative methods have received less research attention [*see box on page 110*]. If a treatment is absent from the list, it means one of two things: either studies have shown that the treatment does not work, or it has not been tested and, therefore, we do not know whether or not it works. Most of the more than 500 "brands" of psychotherapy are not on the EST list, because they fall in the second category.

The Case for ESTs

Advocates have advanced three major arguments in favor of a list of efficacious therapies for specific disorders: it protects patients against fringe psychotherapies, it empowers mental health consumers to make appropriate choices for their care, and it aids in training future therapists.

First, in recent years consumers have been beset by a seemingly endless parade of fad therapies of various stripes [see box on page 111]. Despite scant scientific support—or sometimes outright debunking—some fringe treatments continue to be used widely. For example, surveys of doctoral-level therapists in the 1990s indicated that about one quarter regularly employed two or more recovered-memory techniques. Facilitated communication, discredited by scientific research in the 1990s, is still popular in some communities. Counselors who administer crisis debriefing number in the thousands; in the aftermath of the September 11 terrorist attacks, one crisis-debriefing outfit in Atlanta alone dispatched therapists to 200 companies. All these treatments have been found to be ineffective or even harmful. Some studies have discovered that crisis debriefing, for example, increased the risk of post-traumatic stress disorder in trauma-exposed individuals. The EST list makes it harder for practitioners who administer these and other questionable techniques to claim that they are operating scientifically.

Second, the EST list benefits patients because by providing them with information regarding which treatments have been proven to work, it puts them in a better position to make good choices for their care. Like the Food and Drug Administration's list of approved medications, the EST list performs a quality-control function. It serves a similar purpose for managed care organizations and health care agencies, which want to make scientifically informed decisions about which treatments should—and should not—be reimbursed. By placing the burden of proof on a treatment's proponents to show that it is efficacious, the EST list helps to ensure that therapies promoted to the general public have met basic standards.

Third, the EST list can improve the education and training of graduate students in clinical psychology, social work and other mental health fields. The sprawling psychotherapy research literature is often confusing and contradictory; without such a list, novice clinicians have no clear research guidance concerning which treatments to administer and which to avoid.

The Case against ESTs

Critics have responded with four concerns: EST research findings may not apply to psychotherapy as practiced in the "real world"; the list may be biased toward cognitive-behavioral therapies; the EST view of psychotherapy is narrow; and techniques emphasized by such lists may not be the key ingredients of therapeutic change.

First, critics have attacked ESTs for both the science underlying their "empirical support" and their applicability to clinical practice. "The move to worship at the altar of these scientific treatments has been destructive to clients in practice, because the methods tell you very little about how to read the real and complex people who actually come in for therapy," said psychiatrist Glen O. Gabbard of the Baylor College of Medicine in a 2004 New York Times article.

To satisfy requirements for good research, which seeks to eliminate any variables that could confound the results, investigators must sacrifice a great deal of what practicing psychotherapists believe is important. EST manuals often sharply constrain therapists' flexibility to tailor the treatments to clients' needs, resulting in a one-size-fits-all approach. Researchers reject up to 90 percent of subjects who are initially recruited, in the name of ensuring a "pure" group with the diagnosis of interest. As a result, participants in these studies typically represent only a small percentage of those who might be seen in actual practice.

The all-or-none nature of the EST list also has been criticized. By categorizing treatments as either empirically supported or not, the list omits potentially useful information, such as the degree of efficacy of different EST therapies. Further, many of the ESTs have modest or even rela-

> **Many therapies leave clients slightly better or not helped at all. Can we call them "empirically supported"?**

tively weak effects. That is, they leave many clients slightly improved or not helped at all, with a high likelihood of relapse. Is it reasonable to call such therapies "empirically supported"?

In 2001 psychotherapy researchers Drew Westen, now at Emory University, and Catherine M. Novotny, now at the Department of Veterans Affairs Medical Center in San Francisco, published an analysis of a large number of efficacy studies for depression and some anxiety disorders. Most of the therapies they examined were variants of cognitive-behavioral therapy. Their findings revealed a glass that is both half-full and half-empty.

Third, ESTs focus almost exclusively on symptoms and distress to the exclusion of other important factors that lead people to seek therapy. These considerations include predispositions, vulnerabilities and personality characteristics that often persist after the symptoms are gone. Many psychotherapists believe that it is important to focus on these types of problems in therapy, in order to enhance the quality of the client's life and help reduce the chances of a relapse. The emphasis of ESTs on standardized techniques similarly ignores not only the uniqueness of individuals but also the salutary power of the therapist-client relationship.

> The EST movement has placed evidence-based practice squarely on the agenda of clinical psychology.

On the positive side, they learned that 51 percent of depressed clients and 63 percent of those with panic disorder were significantly better or no longer had symptoms. But the glass seems emptier if we recognize that many patients who had improved still exhibited symptoms at the end of treatment and that others were not helped at all. If we include people who dropped out of therapy, the success percentages plunge considerably. In addition, follow-up studies reveal high rates of relapse. For example, only 37 percent of those depressed clients who completed treatment remained improved one to two years later.

Second, some critics have argued that EST therapies are biased in favor of cognitive-behavioral techniques. Reviews of research on psychoanalytic and humanistic therapies suggest positive effects broadly comparable to those of cognitive-behavioral therapies. Although less research has been conducted on these therapies than on cognitive-behavioral therapy, their underrepresentation on EST lists raises questions of bias.

Fourth, the techniques emphasized by the EST list may not be what produces change in many cases. Most studies comparing the efficacy of two or more therapies find that they all do about equally well. This surprising result is termed the "Dodo Bird verdict," after the Dodo Bird in *Alice's Adventures in Wonderland*, who declares (following a race) that "everybody has won and all must have prizes." Psychotherapy researchers intensely debate the meaning of the Dodo Bird verdict. Some argue that actual important differences exist among therapies but that problems with study design have masked them. Such problems include small samples and the limited range of therapies that have been compared. It is also possible that although average outcomes of various therapies may not differ, some clients may do better with one therapy, whereas other clients may do better with another.

Still other researchers have accepted the Dodo Bird verdict and attempted to account for it. One explanation suggests that therapeutic change is caused more by "common factors" that therapies share rather than by specific techniques. Such factors include instilling hope and providing a believable theoretical rationale with associated therapeutic "rituals," which can make clients feel that they are taking positive action to solve their problems. This perspective also emphasizes the healing power of the therapist-patient relationship.

Future Directions
The EST movement has succeeded in placing the importance of evidence-based practice

(The Authors)

HAL ARKOWITZ and **SCOTT O. LILIENFELD** hope to bring some insights to the contentious discussion surrounding empirically supported therapies. Arkowitz, associate professor of psychology at the University of Arizona, has served as editor of the *Journal of Psychotherapy Integration*. He has received two awards from the Arizona State Psychological Association for distinguished contributions to the practice of psychology and distinguished contributions to the science of psychology. Lilienfeld, associate professor in the department of psychology at Emory University, is former president of the Society for a Science of Clinical Psychology and editor of *Scientific Review of Mental Health Practice*.

Research-Supported Therapies

Below are selected therapies deemed "empirically supported" by the American Psychological Association Division 12 Committee.

THERAPY AND PROBLEM	DESCRIPTION OF THERAPY
Behavior therapy for depression	■ Monitor and increase positive daily activities ■ Improve communication skills ■ Increase assertive behaviors ■ Increase positive reinforcement for nondepressed behaviors ■ Decrease negative life stresses
Cognitive-behavior therapy for depression	■ Teach clients to identify, reevaluate and change overly negative thinking associated with depressed feelings ■ Conduct between-session experiments to test thoughts for accuracy ■ Monitor and increase daily activities
Interpersonal therapy for depression	■ Help clients identify and resolve interpersonal difficulties associated with depression
Cognitive-behavior therapy for bulimia	■ Teach ways to prevent binge eating and create alternative behaviors ■ Develop a plan for a regular pattern of eating ■ Support skills to deal with high-risk situations for binge eating and purging ■ Modify attitudes toward eating and one's physical appearance
Cognitive-behavior therapy for panic disorder	■ Induce panic attacks during sessions to help clients perceive them as less "dangerous" (to reassure them that they will not, for example, "go crazy" or die) ■ Introduce breathing retraining to prevent hyperventilation ■ Control exposure to situations that trigger panic attacks

squarely on the agenda of clinical psychology. Because EST lists have many inherent problems, however, they may prove more useful as a catalyst for helping the field move toward scientifically informed practice than they will be as the final word.

Several promising proposals recently have attempted to refine or replace ESTs in ways that retain their emphasis on science-based practice. One comes from the work of University of New Mexico psychologist William R. Miller. Miller constructed a list of all researched therapies for alcoholism, ranking them by the quality of the research and magnitude of the effects. His method provides access to all relevant information about all therapies studied, not just those that meet the all-or-none criteria for inclusion on the EST list.

Others have suggested that we seek empirically based "principles of change" rather than empirically supported therapies. For example, repeated exposure to feared objects and events is a central principle underlying most effective

Major Approaches to Psychotherapy

More than 500 "brands" of psychotherapy exist. Below is a sampler.

TYPE OF THERAPY	SUBTYPES	VIEW OF CLINICAL PROBLEMS	THERAPY STRATEGIES
Cognitive-behavior	Behavior Cognitive	Result from dysfunctional learning and thinking	Encourage and teach new behaviors; teach people to challenge and correct dysfunctional thinking
Psychoanalytic	Classic Freudian Object relations Self-psychological Relational	Conscious or unconscious psychological conflicts; problems in self-regulation of emotions and impulses; problematic ways of thinking and feeling about the self and others	Help make unconscious processes and conflicts conscious; encourage examination of problematic interpersonal patterns in and out of therapy; teach understanding of how these patterns developed but are no longer adaptive in the present; work to correct these patterns as they are manifested in the therapy relationship
Humanistic-experiential	Client-centered Gestalt Process-experiential Existential	Result from obstacles to the innate growth (self-actualization) processes of being human	Support the client's experience of understanding, caring and empathy, leading to changed views of the self; introduce exercises to provide opportunities that increase awareness of feelings and that facilitate change
Integrative	*Theoretical integration:* Integrating two or more therapies *Systematic eclecticism:* Selecting and matching treatment to the person and problem *Common factors:* Combining the factors that different therapies share	Incorporate all major psychotherapies and ways of understanding clinical problems	Draw from any existing therapy approaches

treatments for anxiety disorders. Therapists can derive many ways of flexibly implementing a principle of change to fit clients without being constrained by a specific technique or manual. In a similar vein, others have recently suggested that we focus on "empirically supported relationship factors," such as therapist empathy and warmth. But there is not yet sufficient agreement concerning which change or relationship principles should qualify as empirically supported.

Another alternative to ESTs was proposed by a committee appointed by past APA president Ronald F. Levant. The concept, which is called evidence-based practice, has been widely embraced in many areas of medicine. In its 2005 policy statement, the APA committee defined evidence-based practice as "the integration of the best available research with clinical expertise in the context of patient characteristics, culture, and preferences."

The term "best available research" is much broader than evidence based on psychotherapy studies alone. It encompasses research across the entire field of psychology, including personality, psychopathology and social psychology. "Clinical expertise" relates to therapist competencies that are not tied directly to research but that are believed to promote positive therapeutic outcomes. These capabilities inform the ability to form therapeutic relationships with clients and to devise and implement treatment plans. Finally, inclusion of client characteristics, culture and preferences points to the importance of tailoring treatments to individuals.

Although this APA report is a noble effort to grapple with some of the controversies, its long-term impact remains unclear. Many EST proponents have been dissatisfied with the recommendation to employ "the best available research" as being so vague, at least compared with the specificity of ESTs, as to be of little value. Many EST advocates have also objected to the inclusion of clinical expertise in a definition of evidence-based practice.

Given the shortcomings of ESTs and the existing alternatives to them, it is clear that the field is just beginning to incorporate science-based practice. Nevertheless, we can begin to see the broad outlines of promising positions that are less dogmatic than earlier ones. Such trends

Therapies to Avoid?

A selective sampling of treatments for which there is scant scientific support.

- **Energy therapies**
  Purport to treat clients' anxiety disorders by manipulating their invisible energy fields

- **Recovered-memory techniques**
  Suggestive methods (such as hypnosis, guided imagery, keeping journals) designed to unearth "memories" of early child abuse

- **Rebirthing therapies**
  Claimed to treat adolescents' and younger children's anger by forcing them to reenact the trauma of birth

- **Facilitated communication**
  Said to allow mute autistic children to type sentences on a computer keyboard with the aid of an assistant who guides their hand movements

- **Crisis debriefing**
  Intended to ward off post-traumatic stress disorder in trauma victims by strongly encouraging them to "process" the emotions and memories associated with the anxiety-provoking event, even if they do not feel ready to do so

may help assuage the legitimate concerns of both researchers and practitioners. Ultimately we believe that the field must move beyond a narrow definition of ESTs toward views that bridge the gap between researchers and practitioners. After all, whatever their differences may be, aren't all clinical psychologists seeking better ways to help troubled people feel happier and live enriching lives? **M**

(Further Reading)

◆ The Great Psychotherapy Debate: Models, Methods, and Findings. Bruce E. Wampold. Lawrence Erlbaum Associates, 2001.
◆ Evidence-Based Practices in Mental Health: Debate and Dialogue on the Fundamental Questions. Edited by John C. Norcross, L. E. Beutler and R. F. Levant. American Psychological Association Press, 2005.

By Robert B. Cialdini

the SCIENCE of Persuasion

Social psychology has determined the basic principles that govern getting to "yes"

Hello there.

I hope you've enjoyed the magazine so far. Now I'd like to let you in on something of great importance to you personally. Have you ever been tricked into saying yes? Ever felt trapped into buying something you didn't really want or contributing to some suspicious-sounding cause? And have you ever wished you understood why you acted in this way so that you could withstand these clever ploys in the future?

Yes? Then clearly this article is just right for you. It contains valuable information on the most powerful psychological pressures that get you to say yes to requests. And it's chock-full of NEW, IMPROVED *research showing exactly how and why these techniques work. So don't delay, just settle in and get the information that, after all, you've already agreed you want.*

The scientific study of the process of social influence has been under way for well over half a century, beginning in earnest with the propaganda, public information and persuasion programs of World War II. Since that time, numerous social scientists have investigated the ways in which one individual can influence another's attitudes and actions. For the past 30 years, I have participated in that endeavor, concentrating primarily on the major factors that bring about a specific form of behavior change—compliance with a request. Six basic tendencies of human behavior come into play in generating a positive response: recip-rocation, consistency, social validation, liking, authority and scarcity. As these six tendencies help to govern our business dealings, our societal involvements and our personal relationships, knowledge of the rules of persuasion can truly be thought of as empowerment.

Reciprocation

When the Disabled American Veterans organization mails out requests for contributions, the appeal succeeds only about 18 percent of the time. But when the mailing includes a set of free personalized address labels, the success rate almost doubles, to 35 percent. To understand the effect of

the unsolicited gift, we must recognize the reach and power of an essential rule of human conduct: the code of reciprocity.

All societies subscribe to a norm that obligates individuals to repay in kind what they have received. Evolutionary selection pressure has probably entrenched the behavior in social animals such as ourselves. The demands of reciprocity begin to explain the boost in donations to the veterans group. Receiving a gift—unsolicited and perhaps even unwanted—convinced significant numbers of potential donors to return the favor.

Charitable organizations are far from alone in taking this approach: food stores offer free samples, exterminators offer free in-home inspections,

health clubs offer free workouts. Customers are thus exposed to the product or service, but they are also indebted. Consumers are not the only ones who fall under the sway of reciprocity. Pharmaceutical companies spend millions of dollars every year to support medical researchers and to provide gifts to individual physicians—activities that may subtly influence investigators' findings and physicians' recommendations. A 1998 study in the *New England Journal of Medicine* found that only 37 percent of researchers who published conclusions critical of the safety of calcium channel blockers had previously received drug company support. Among those whose conclusions attested to the drugs' safety, however, the number of

Free samples carry a subtle price tag; they psychologically indebt the consumer to reciprocate. Here shoppers get complimentary tastes of a new product, green ketchup.

Public commitment of signing a petition influences the signer to behave consistently with that position in the future.

those who had received free trips, research funding or employment skyrocketed—to 100 percent.

Reciprocity includes more than gifts and favors; it also applies to concessions that people make to one another. For example, assume that you reject my large request, and I then make a concession to you by retreating to a smaller request. You may very well then reciprocate with a concession of your own: agreement with my lesser request. In the mid-1970s my colleagues and I conducted an experiment that clearly illustrates the dynamics of reciprocal concessions. We stopped a random sample of passersby on public walkways and asked them if they would volunteer to chaperone juvenile detention center inmates on a day trip to the zoo. As expected, very few complied, only 17 percent.

For another random sample of passersby, however, we began with an even larger request: to serve as an unpaid counselor at the center for two hours per week for the next two years. Everyone in this second sampling rejected the extreme appeal. At that point we offered them a concession. "If you can't do that," we asked, "would you chaperone a group of juvenile detention center inmates on a day trip to the zoo?" Our concession powerfully stimulated return concessions. The compliance rate nearly tripled, to 50 percent, compared with the straightforward zoo-trip request.

Consistency

In 1998 Gordon Sinclair, the owner of a well-known Chicago restaurant, was struggling with a problem that afflicts all restaurateurs. Patrons frequently reserve a table but, without notice, fail to appear. Sinclair solved the problem by asking his receptionist to change two words of what she said to callers requesting reservations. The change dropped his no-call, no-show rate from 30 to 10 percent immediately.

The two words were effective because they commissioned the force of another potent human motivation: the desire to be, and to appear, consistent. The receptionist merely modified her request from "Please call if you have to change your plans" to "Will you please call if you have to change your plans?" At that point, she politely paused and waited for a response. The wait was pivotal because it induced customers to fill the pause with a public commitment. And public commitments, even seemingly minor ones, direct future action.

In another example, Joseph Schwarzwald of

Bar-Ilan University in Israel and his co-workers nearly doubled monetary contributions for the handicapped in certain neighborhoods. The key factor: two weeks before asking for contributions, they got residents to sign a petition supporting the handicapped, thus making a public commitment to that same cause.

Social Validation

On a wintry morning in the late 1960s, a man stopped on a busy New York City sidewalk and gazed skyward for 60 seconds, at nothing in particular. He did so as part of an experiment by City University of New York social psychologists Stanley Milgram, Leonard Bickman and Lawrence Berkowitz that was designed to find out what effect this action would have on passersby. Most simply detoured or brushed by; 4 percent joined the man in looking up. The experiment was then repeated with a slight change. With the modification, large numbers of pedestrians were induced to come to a halt, crowd together and peer upward.

The single alteration in the experiment incorporated the phenomenon of social validation. One fundamental way that we decide what to do in a situation is to look to what others are doing or have done there. If many individuals have decided in favor of a particular idea, we are more likely to follow, because we perceive the idea to be more correct, more valid.

Milgram, Bickman and Berkowitz introduced the influence of social validation into their street experiment simply by having five men rather than one look up at nothing. With the larger initial set of upward gazers, the percentage of New Yorkers who followed suit more than quadrupled, to 18 percent. Bigger initial sets of planted up-lookers generated an even greater response: a starter group of 15 led 40 percent of passersby to join in, nearly stopping traffic within one minute.

Taking advantage of social validation, requesters can stimulate our compliance by demonstrating (or merely implying) that others just like us have already complied. For example, a study found that a fund-raiser who showed homeowners a list of neighbors who had donated to a local charity significantly increased the frequency of contributions; the longer the list, the greater the effect. Marketers, therefore, go out of their way to inform us when their product is the largest-selling or fastest-growing of its kind, and television commercials regularly depict crowds rushing to stores to acquire the advertised item.

Less obvious, however, are the circumstances under which social validation can backfire to pro-

duce the opposite of what a requester intends. An example is the understandable but potentially misguided tendency of health educators to call attention to a problem by depicting it as regrettably frequent. Information campaigns stress that alcohol and drug use is intolerably high, that adolescent suicide rates are alarming and that polluters are spoiling the environment. Although the claims are both true and well intentioned, the creators of these campaigns have missed something basic about the compliance process. Within the statement "Look at all the people who are doing this *undesirable* thing" lurks the powerful and undercutting message "Look at all the people who *are* doing this undesirable thing." Research shows that, as a consequence, many such programs boomerang, generating even more of the undesirable behavior.

For instance, a suicide intervention program administered to New Jersey teenagers informed them of the high number of teenage suicides. Health researcher David Shaffer and his colleagues at Columbia University found that participants became significantly more likely to see suicide as a potential solution to their problems. Of greater effectiveness are campaigns that honestly depict the unwanted activity as damaging despite the fact that relatively few individuals engage in it.

Liking

"Affinity," "rapport" and "affection" all describe a feeling of connection between people. But the simple word "liking" most faithfully captures the concept and has become the standard designation in the social science literature. People prefer to say yes to those they like. Consider the worldwide success of the Tupperware Corporation and its "home party" program. Through the in-home demonstration get-together, the company arranges for its customers to buy from a liked friend, the host, rather than from an unknown salesperson. So favorable has been the effect on proceeds that, according to company literature, a Tupperware party begins somewhere in the world every two seconds. In fact, 75 percent of all Tupperware parties today occur outside the individualistic U.S., in countries where group social bonding is even more important than it is here.

Of course, most commercial transactions take place beyond the homes of friends. Under these much more typical circumstances, those who wish to commission the power of liking employ tactics clustered around certain factors that research has shown to work.

Physical attractiveness can be such a tool. In a

This year Americans will produce more litter and pollution than ever before.

If you don't do something about it, who will?

Give A Hoot. Don't Pollute.

Forest Service-USDA

Social validation takes advantage of peer pressure to drive human behavior. Poorly applied, however, it can also undermine attempts to curtail deleterious activities, by pointing out their ubiquity: If everyone's doing it, why shouldn't I?

1993 study conducted by Peter H. Reingen of Arizona State University and Jerome B. Kernan, now at George Mason University, good-looking fundraisers for the American Heart Association generated nearly twice as many donations (42 versus 23 percent) as did other requesters. In the 1970s researchers Michael G. Efran and E.W.J. Patterson of the University of Toronto found that voters in Canadian federal elections gave physically

quests, the amount of the donations more than doubled.

Compliments also stimulate liking, and direct salespeople are trained in the use of praise. Indeed, even inaccurate praise may be effective. Research at the University of North Carolina at Chapel Hill found that compliments produced just as much liking for the flatterer when they were untrue as when they were genuine.

(Are we then doomed to be helplessly manipulated by these principles? No.)

attractive candidates several times as many votes as unattractive ones. Yet such voters insisted that their choices would never be influenced by something as superficial as appearance.

Similarity also can expedite the development of rapport. Salespeople often search for, or outright fabricate, a connection between themselves and their customers: "Well, no kidding, you're from Minneapolis? I went to school in Minnesota!" Fund-raisers do the same, with good results. In 1994 psychologists R. Kelly Aune of the University of Hawaii at Manoa and Michael D. Basil of the University of Denver reported research in which solicitors canvassed a college campus asking for contributions to a charity. When the phrase "I'm a student, too" was added to the re-

Cooperation is another factor that has been shown to enhance positive feelings and behavior. Salespeople, for example, often strive to be perceived by their prospects as cooperating partners. Automobile sales managers frequently cast themselves as "villains" so the salesperson can "do battle" on the customer's behalf. The gambit naturally leads to a desirable form of liking by the customer for the salesperson, which promotes sales.

Authority

Recall the man who used social validation to get large numbers of passersby to stop and stare at the sky. He might achieve the opposite effect and spur stationary strangers into motion by assuming the mantle of authority. In 1955 University of Texas at Austin researchers Monroe Lefkowitz, Robert R. Blake and Jane S. Mouton discovered that a man could increase by 350 percent the number of pedestrians who would follow him across the street against the light by changing one simple thing. Instead of casual dress, he donned markers of authority: a suit and tie.

Those touting their experience, expertise or scientific credentials may be trying to harness the power of authority: "Babies are our business, our only business," "Four out of five doctors recommend," and so on. (The author's biography on the opposite page in part serves such a purpose.) There is nothing wrong with such claims when they are real, because we usually want the opinions of true authorities. Their insights help us choose quickly and well.

The problem comes when we are subjected to phony claims. If we fail to think, as is often the case when confronted by authority symbols, we can easily be steered in the wrong direction by ersatz experts—those who merely present the aura of legitimacy. That Texas jaywalker in a suit and tie was no more an authority on crossing the street

Behold the power of authority. Certainly not lost on the National Rifle Association is that the authority inherent in such heroic figures as Moses, El Cid and Ben-Hur is linked to the actor who portrayed them, Charlton Heston.

than the rest of the pedestrians who nonetheless followed him. A highly successful ad campaign in the 1970s featured actor Robert Young proclaiming the health benefits of decaffeinated coffee. Young seems to have been able to dispense this medical opinion effectively because he represented, at the time, the nation's most famous physician. That Marcus Welby, M.D., was only a character on a TV show was less important than the appearance of authority.

Scarcity

While at Florida State University in the 1970s, psychologist Stephen West noted an odd occurrence after surveying students about the campus cafeteria cuisine: ratings of the food rose significantly from the week before, even though there had been no change in the menu, food quality or preparation. Instead the shift resulted from an announcement that because of a fire, cafeteria meals would not be available for several weeks.

This account highlights the effect of perceived scarcity on human judgment. A great deal of evidence shows that items and opportunities become more desirable to us as they become less available.

For this reason, marketers trumpet the unique benefits or the one-of-a-kind character of their offerings. It is also for this reason that they consistently engage in "limited time only" promotions or put us into competition with one another using sales campaigns based on "limited supply."

Less widely recognized is that scarcity affects the value not only of commodities but of information as well. Information that is exclusive is more persuasive. Take as evidence the dissertation data of a former student of mine, Amram Knishinsky, who owned a company that imported beef into the U.S. and sold it to supermarkets. To examine the effects of scarcity and exclusivity on compliance, he instructed his telephone sales-

Friends (who are already liked) are powerful salespeople, as Tupperware Corporation discovered. Strangers can co-opt the trappings of friendship to encourage compliance.

(The Author)

ROBERT B. CIALDINI is Regents' Professor of Psychology at Arizona State University, where he has also been named Distinguished Graduate Research Professor. He is past president of the Society of Personality and Social Psychology. Cialdini's book *Influence*, which was the result of a three-year study of the reasons why people comply with requests in everyday settings, has appeared in numerous editions and been published in nine languages. He attributes his long-standing interest in the intricacies of influence to the fact that he was raised in an entirely Italian family, in a predominantly Polish neighborhood, in a historically German city (Milwaukee), in an otherwise rural state.

people to call a randomly selected sample of customers and to make a standard request of them to purchase beef. He also instructed the salespeople to do the same with a second random sample of customers but to add that a shortage of Australian beef was anticipated, which was true, because of certain weather conditions there. The added information that Australian beef was soon to be scarce more than doubled purchases.

Finally, he had his staff call a third sample of customers, to tell them (1) about the impending shortage of Australian beef and (2) that this information came from his company's *exclusive* sources in the Australian national weather service. These customers increased their orders by more than 600 percent. They were influenced by a scarcity double whammy: not only was the beef scarce, but the information that the beef was scarce was itself scarce.

Knowledge Is Power

I think it noteworthy that many of the data presented in this article have come from studies of the practices of persuasion professionals—the marketers, advertisers, salespeople, fund-raisers and their comrades whose financial well-being de-

(Influence across Cultures)

D o the six key factors in the social influence process operate similarly across national boundaries? Yes, but with a wrinkle. The citizens of the world are human, after all, and susceptible to the fundamental tendencies that characterize all members of our species. Cultural norms, traditions and experiences can, however, modify the weight that is brought to bear by each factor.

Consider the results of a report published in 2000 by Stanford University's Michael W. Morris, Joel M. Podolny and Sheira Ariel, who studied employees of Citibank, a multinational financial corporation. The researchers selected four societies for examination: the U.S., China, Spain and Germany. They surveyed Citibank branches within each country and measured employees' willingness to comply voluntarily with a request from a co-worker for assistance with a task. Although multiple key factors could come into play, the main reason employees felt obligated to comply differed in the four nations. Each of these reasons incorporated a different fundamental principle of social influence.

Employees in the U.S. took a reciprocation-based approach to the decision to comply. They asked the question, "What has this person done for me recently?" and felt obligated to volunteer if they owed the requester a favor. Chinese employees responded primarily to authority, in the form of loyalties to those of high status within their small group. They asked, "Is this requester connected to someone in my unit, especially someone who is high-ranking?" If the answer was yes, they felt required to yield.

Spanish Citibank personnel based the deci-

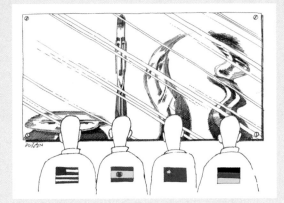

Cultural norms can alter perceptions of persuasion tactics.

sion to comply mostly on liking/friendship. They were willing to help on the basis of friendship norms that encourage faithfulness to one's friends, regardless of position or status. They asked, "Is this requester connected to my friends?" If the answer was yes, they were especially likely to want to comply.

German employees were most compelled by consistency, offering assistance in order to be consistent with the rules of the organization. They decided whether to comply by asking, "According to official regulations and categories, am I supposed to assist this requester?" If the answer was yes, they felt a strong obligation to grant the request.

In sum, although all human societies seem to play by the same set of influence rules, the weights assigned to the various rules can differ across cultures. Persuasive appeals to audiences in distinct cultures need to take such differences into account. —*R.B.C.*